Dover Thrift Study Edition

As You Like It

WILLIAM SHAKESPEARE

DOVER PUBLICATIONS, INC.
Mineola, New York

Copyright

Bibliographical Note

This Dover edition, first published in 2011, contains the unabridged text of *As You Like It,* as published in Volume V of *The Caxton Edition of the Complete Works of William Shakespeare,* Caxton Publishing Company, London, n.d., plus literary analysis and perspectives from *MAXnotes® for As You Like It,* published in 1996 by Research & Education Association, Inc., Piscataway, New Jersey.

Library of Congress Cataloging-in-Publication Data

Shakespeare, William, 1564–1616.
   As you like it / William Shakespeare.
      p. cm. — (Dover thrift study editions)
   Includes bibliographical references.
   ISBN-13: 978-0-486-48250-7
   ISBN-10: 0-486-48250-2
   1. Fathers and daughters—Drama. 2. Exiles—Drama. I. Title.

PR2803.A1 2011
822.3'3—dc22

2010052833

Manufactured in the United States by Courier Corporation
48250201
www.doverpublications.com

Publisher's Note

Combining the complete text of a classic novel or drama with a comprehensive study guide, Dover Thrift Study Editions are the most effective way to gain a thorough understanding of the major works of world literature.

The study guide features up-to-date and expert analysis of every chapter or section from the source work. Questions and fully explained answers follow, allowing readers to analyze the material critically. Character lists, author bios, and discussions of the work's historical context are also provided.

Each Dover Thrift Study Edition includes everything a student needs to prepare for homework, discussions, reports, and exams.

Contents

As You Like It

WILLIAM SHAKESPEARE

Contents

Contents

Dramatis Personæ[1]

DUKE, living in banishment.
FREDERICK, his brother, and usurper of his dominions.
AMIENS,
JAQUES, } lords attending on the banished Duke.
LE BEAU, a courtier attending upon Frederick.
CHARLES, wrestler to Frederick.
OLIVER,
JAQUES, } sons of Sir Rowland de Boys.
ORLANDO,
ADAM,
DENNIS, } servants to Oliver.
TOUCHSTONE, a clown.
SIR OLIVER MARTEXT, a vicar.
CORIN,
SYLVIUS, } shepherds.
WILLIAM, a country fellow, in love with Audrey.
A person representing Hymen.

ROSALIND, daughter to the banished Duke.
CELIA, daughter to Frederick.
PHEBE, a shepherdess.
AUDREY, a country wench.

Lords, pages, and attendants, &c.

SCENE—*Oliver's house; Duke Frederick's court; and the Forest of Arden*

[1]This play, which was first printed in the First Folio in 1623, is there divided into acts
and scenes. There is no list of *Dramatis Personæ*. This was supplied for the first time
in Rowe's edition of 1709.

Dramatis Personæ

DUKE, living in banishment.

FREDERICK, his brother, and usurper of his dominions.

AMIENS, } lords attending on the banished Duke.
JAQUES }

LE BEAU, a courtier attending upon Frederick.

CHARLES, wrestler to Frederick.

OLIVER, }
JAQUES, } sons of Sir Rowland de Boys.
ORLANDO,}

ADAM, } servants to Oliver.
DENNIS,}

TOUCHSTONE, a clown.

SIR OLIVER MARTEXT, a vicar.

CORIN, } shepherds.
SILVIUS,}

WILLIAM, a country fellow, in love with Audrey.

A person representing Hymen.

ROSALIND, daughter to the banished Duke.

CELIA, daughter to Frederick.

PHEBE, a shepherdess.

AUDREY, a country wench.

Lords, pages, and attendants, &c.

SCENE: Oliver's house; Duke Frederick's court; and the Forest of Arden.

This play, which was first printed in the First Folio of 1623, is there divided into acts and scenes. There is no list of Dramatis Personæ. This was supplied for the first time by Mr. Rowe, editor of 1709.

ACT I.

SCENE I. *Orchard of Oliver's House.*

Enter ORLANDO *and* ADAM

ORLANDO.   As I remember, Adam, it was upon this fashion: bequeathed me[1] by will but poor a thousand crowns, and, as thou
sayest, charged my brother, on his blessing, to breed me well: and
there begins my sadness. My brother Jaques[2] he keeps at school,
and report speaks goldenly of his profit: for my part, he keeps me
rustically at home, or, to speak more properly, stays me here at
home unkept; for call you that keeping for a gentleman of my
birth, that differs not from the stalling of an ox? His horses are bred
better; for, besides that they are fair with their feeding, they are
taught their manage, and to that end riders dearly hired: but I, his
brother, gain nothing under him but growth; for the which his animals on his dunghills are as much bound to him as I. Besides this
nothing that he so plentifully gives me, the something that nature
gave me his countenance[3] seems to take from me: he lets me feed
with his hinds, bars me the place of a brother, and, as much as in

---

[1]*bequeathed me, etc.*] This sentence lacks a subject. It is possible that "he" was omitted
before "bequeathed" by a typographical error. It is so obvious that Orlando is talking
of his father's bequest that a corrector of the press could not be severely blamed for the
accidental elision.

[2]*My brother Jaques*] This character, Sir Rowland de Boys' second son, only plays a small
part at the end of the last act, where the folio editions call him "second brother" and
Rowe and later editors "Jaques de Boys." In Lodge's story of *Rosalynd,* on which
Shakespeare based his play, the character is called Ferdinand. That Shakespeare
should have bestowed the same name on a far more important personage of his own
creation, the banished Duke's cynical companion, is proof of hasty composition and of
defective revision. Cf. note on I, ii, 74, *infra.*

[3]*countenance*] Cf. Selden's *Table Talk* (Art. "Fines"): "If you will come unto my house,
I will show you the best *countenance* I can," *i.e.* not the best face, but the best
entertainment.

1

him lies, mines my gentility with my education.[4] This is it, Adam, that grieves me; and the spirit of my father, which I think is within me, begins to mutiny against this servitude: I will no longer endure it, though yet I know no wise remedy how to avoid it.

ADAM.   Yonder comes my master, your brother.

ORL.   Go apart, Adam, and thou shalt hear how he will shake me up.

Enter OLIVER

OLI.   Now, sir! what make you here?

ORL.   Nothing: I am not taught to make any thing.

OLI.   What mar you then, sir?

ORL.   Marry, sir, I am helping you to mar that which God made, a poor unworthy brother of yours, with idleness.

OLI.   Marry, sir, be better employed, and be naught awhile.[5]

ORL.   Shall I keep your hogs and eat husks with them? What prodigal portion have I spent, that I should come to such penury?

OLI.   Know you where you are, sir?

ORL.   O, sir, very well; here in your orchard.

OLI.   Know you before whom, sir?

ORL.   Ay, better than him I am before knows me. I know you are my eldest brother; and, in the gentle condition of blood, you should so know me. The courtesy of nations allows you my better, in that you are the firstborn; but the same tradition takes not away my blood, were there twenty brothers betwixt us: I have as much of my father in me as you; albeit, I confess, your coming before me is nearer to his reverence.[6]

OLI.   What, boy!

ORL.   Come, come, elder brother, you are too young in this.[7]

OLI.   Wilt thou lay hands on me, villain?

ORL.   I am no villain; I am the youngest son of Sir Rowland de Boys; he was my father, and he is thrice a villain that says such a father begot villains. Wert thou not my brother, I would not take this hand from thy throat till this other had pulled out thy tongue for saying so: thou hast railed on thyself.

---

[4]*mines . . . education*] undermines or destroys the gentleness of my birth and nature, by means of my bringing up.

[5]*be naught awhile*] a colloquial form of imprecation, "be hanged to you."

[6]*your coming . . . reverence*] your priority of birth more closely associates you with the respect which was his due. The chief share of the father's reputation descends to his eldest born.

[7]*Come, come . . . young in this*] Cf. the elder brother's remark in Lodge's story of *Rosalynd*, "Though I am *eldest* by birth, yet never having attempted any deeds of arms, I am *youngest* to perform any martial exploits."

ADAM.   Sweet masters, be patient: for your father's remembrance, be at accord.

OLI.   Let me go, I say.

ORL.   I will not, till I please: you shall hear me. My father charged you in his will to give me good education: you have trained me like a peasant, obscuring and hiding from me all gentleman-like qualities. The spirit of my father grows strong in me, and I will no longer endure it: therefore allow me such exercises as may become a gentleman, or give me the poor allottery my father left me by testament; with that I will go buy my fortunes.

OLI.   And what wilt thou do? beg, when that is spent? Well, sir, get you in: I will not long be troubled with you; you shall have some part of your will: I pray you, leave me.

ORL.   I will no further offend you than becomes me for my good.

OLI.   Get you with him, you old dog.

ADAM.   Is "old dog" my reward?? Most true, I have lost my teeth in your service. God be with my old master! he would not have spoke such a word.

                       [*Exeunt* ORLANDO *and* ADAM.

OLI.   Is it even so? begin you to grow upon me? I will physic your rankness, and yet give no thousand crowns neither. Holla, Dennis!

Enter DENNIS

DEN.   Calls your worship?

OLI.   Was not Charles, the Duke's wrestler, here to speak with me?

DEN.   So please you, he is here at the door and importunes access to you.

OLI.   Call him in. [*Exit* DENNIS.] 'T will be a good way; and tomorrow the wrestling is.

Enter CHARLES

CHA.   Good morrow to your worship.

OLI.   Good Monsieur Charles, what's the new news at the new court?

CHA.   There's no news at the court, sir, but the old news: that is, the old Duke is banished by his younger brother the new Duke; and three or four loving lords have put themselves into voluntary exile with him, whose lands and revenues enrich the new Duke; therefore he gives them good leave to wander.

OLI.   Can you tell if Rosalind, the Duke's daughter, be banished with her father?

CHA.   O, no; for the Duke's daughter, her cousin, so loves her, being ever from their cradles bred together, that she would have followed her exile, or have died to stay behind her. She is at the court, and no less beloved of her uncle than his own daughter; and never two ladies loved as they do.

OLI. Where will the old Duke live?

CHA. They say he is already in the forest of Arden,[8] and a many merry men with him; and there they live like the old Robin Hood of England: they say many young gentlemen flock to him every day, and fleet the time carelessly, as they did in the golden world.

OLI. What, you wrestle to-morrow before the new Duke?

CHA. Marry, do I, sir; and I came to acquaint you with a matter. I am given, sir, secretly to understand that your younger brother, Orlando, hath a disposition to come in disguised against me to try a fall. To-morrow, sir, I wrestle for my credit; and he that escapes me without some broken limb shall acquit him well. Your brother is but young and tender; and, for your love, I would be loath to foil him, as I must, for my own honour, if he come in: therefore, out of my love to you, I came hither to acquaint you withal; that either you might stay him from his intendment, or brook such disgrace well as he shall run into; in that it is a thing of his own search, and altogether against my will.

OLI. Charles, I thank thee for thy love to me, which thou shalt find I will most kindly requite. I had myself notice of my brother's purpose herein, and have by underhand means laboured to dissuade him from it, but he is resolute. I'll tell thee, Charles:—it is the stubbornest young fellow of France; full of ambition, an envious emulator of every man's good parts, a secret and villanous contriver against me his natural brother: therefore use thy discretion; I had as lief thou didst break his neck as his finger. And thou wert best look to 't; for if thou dost him any slight disgrace, or if he do not mightily grace himself on thee,[9] he will practise against thee by poison, entrap thee by some treacherous device, and never leave thee till he hath ta'en thy life by some indirect means or other; for, I assure thee, and almost with tears I speak it, there is not one so young and so villanous this day living. I speak but brotherly of him; but should I anatomize him to thee as he is, I must blush and weep, and thou must look pale and wonder.

CHA. I am heartily glad I came hither to you. If he come to-morrow, I'll give him his payment: if ever he go alone again, I'll never wrestle for prize more: and so, God keep your worship!

---

[8] *forest of Arden*] Lodge, like Shakespeare, makes the scene of his story "the forest of *Ardennes*," in Flanders (now Belgium). But the dramatist's familiarity with the English forest of *Arden* in Warwickshire, near his native town of Stratford-on-Avon, probably coloured his allusions to woodland scenery in the play.

[9] *grace himself on thee*] get grace or honour at your expense.

OLI. Farewell, good Charles. [*Exit* CHARLES.] Now will I stir this
gamester: I hope I shall see an end of him; for my soul, yet I know
not why, hates nothing more than he. Yet he's gentle; never
schooled, and yet learned; full of noble device;[10] of all sorts enchantingly beloved; and indeed so much in the heart of the world,
and especially of my own people, who best know him, that I am
altogether misprised: but it shall not be so long; this wrestler shall
clear all: nothing remains but that I kindle the boy thither; which
now I'll go about.   [*Exit.*

SCENE II. *Lawn Before the Duke's Palace.*

Enter ROSALIND *and* CELIA

CEL. I pray thee, Rosalind, sweet my coz, be merry.
ROS. Dear Celia, I show more mirth than I am mistress of; and would
you yet I were merrier? Unless you could teach me to forget a banished father, you must not learn me how to remember any extraordinary pleasure.
CEL. Herein I see thou lovest me not with the full weight that I love
thee. If my uncle, thy banished father, had banished thy uncle, the
Duke my father, so thou hadst been still with me, I could have
taught my love to take thy father for mine: so wouldst thou, if the
truth of thy love to me were so righteously tempered as mine is to
thee.
ROS. Well, I will forget the condition of my estate, to rejoice in yours.
CEL. You know my father hath no child but I, nor none is like to have:
and, truly, when he dies, thou shalt be his heir; for what he hath
taken away from thy father perforce, I will render thee again in affection; by mine honour, I will; and when I break that oath, let me
turn monster: therefore, my sweet Rose, my dear Rose, be merry.
ROS. From henceforth I will, coz, and devise sports. Let me see; what
think you of falling in love?
CEL. Marry, I prithee, do, to make sport withal: but love no man in
good earnest; nor no further in sport neither, than with safety of a
pure blush thou mayst in honour come off again.
ROS. What shall be our sport, then?

[10]*noble device*] noble conceptions and aims.

CEL. Let us sit and mock the good housewife Fortune from her wheel,[1] that her gifts may henceforth be bestowed equally.

ROS. I would we could do so; for her benefits are mightily misplaced; and the bountiful blind woman doth most mistake in her gifts to women.

CEL. 'T is true; for those that she makes fair she scarce makes honest; and those that she makes honest she makes very ill-favouredly.

ROS. Nay, now thou goest from Fortune's office to Nature's: Fortune reigns in gifts of the world, not in the lineaments of Nature.

Enter TOUCHSTONE

CEL. No? when Nature hath made a fair creature, may she not by Fortune fall into the fire? Though Nature hath given us wit to flout at Fortune, hath not Fortune sent in this fool to cut off the argument?

ROS. Indeed, there is Fortune too hard for Nature, when Fortune makes Nature's natural the cutter-off of Nature's wit.

CEL. Peradventure this is not Fortune's work neither, but Nature's; who perceiveth our natural wits too dull to reason of[2] such goddesses, and hath sent this natural for our whetstone; for always the dulness of the fool is the whetstone of the wits. How now, wit! whither wander you?[3]

TOUCH. Mistress, you must come away to your father.

CEL. Were you made the messenger?

TOUCH. No, by mine honour, but I was bid to come for you.

ROS. Where learned you that oath, fool?

TOUCH. Of a certain knight that swore by his honour they were good pancakes, and swore by his honour the mustard was naught; now I'll stand to it, the pancakes were naught and the mustard was good, and yet was not the knight forsworn.

CEL. How prove you that, in the great heap of your knowledge?

ROS. Ay, marry, now unmuzzle your wisdom.

TOUCH. Stand you both forth now: stroke your chins, and swear by your beards that I am a knave.

CEL. By our beards, if we had them, thou art.

TOUCH. By my knavery, if I had it, then I were; but if you swear by that that is not, you are not forsworn: no more was this knight, swearing by his honour, for he never had any; or if he had, he had sworn it away before ever he saw those pancakes or that mustard.

[1]*Fortune . . . wheel*] Cf. *Hen.* V, III, vi, 32–34: "*Fortune* is painted . . . with a *wheel*, to signify to you, which is the moral of it, that she is turning, and inconstant, and mutability, and variation."
[2]*reason of*] discuss about. Cf. *Merch. of Ven.*, I, iii, 54, "I am debating *of* my present store," and *ibid.* II, viii, 27, "I *reasoned with* a Frenchman yesterday."
[3]*wit! whither wander you?*] a proverbial phrase serving as a check on too abundant a flow of conversation. The cognate form IV, i, 149, *infra*, "Wit! whither wilt?" is more frequently met with. Malone conjectured that the words formed part of some lost madrigal.

CEL.   Prithee, who is 't that thou meanest?

TOUCH.   One that old Frederick, your father,[4] loves.

CEL.   My father's love is enough to honour him: enough! speak no
more of him; you'll be whipped for taxation one of these days.

TOUCH.   The more pity, that fools may not speak wisely what wise
men do foolishly.

CEL.   By my troth, thou sayest true; for since the little wit that fools
have was silenced, the little foolery that wise men have makes a
great show.[5] Here comes Monsieur Le Beau.

ROS.   With his mouth full of news.

CEL.   Which he will put on us, as pigeons feed their young.

ROS.   Then shall we be news-crammed.

CEL.   All the better; we shall be the more marketable.

Enter LE BEAU

Bon jour, Monsieur Le Beau: what's the news?

LE BEAU.   Fair princess, you have lost much good sport.

CEL.   Sport! of what colour?[6]

LE BEAU.   What colour, madam! how shall I answer you?

ROS.   As wit and fortune will.

TOUCH.   Or as the Destinies decrees.

CEL.   Well said: that was laid on with a trowel.

TOUCH.   Nay, if I keep not my rank,—

ROS.   Thou losest thy old smell.[7]

LE BEAU.   You amaze me, ladies: I would have told you of good
wrestling, which you have lost the sight of.

ROS.   Yet tell us the manner of the wrestling.

LE BEAU.   I will tell you the beginning; and, if it please your ladyships,

---

[4] *old Frederick, your father*] The reference here must be to Celia's father, the usurping
Duke, who at line 213 of the present scene and at V, iv, 148, *infra*, is also called
Frederick. Yet the Folios give the succeeding speech to *Rosalind*, and thereby imply that
Touchstone refers here to Rosalind's father, the banished Duke, who is designated
throughout the play as "Duke, senior," without any Christian name; it is clear that his
name could not have been Frederick, like that of his brother. Capell, who accepted the
Folios' assignment of the next speech to Rosalind, substituted Ferdinand for Frederick.
But it is best to adopt Theobald's emendation, which is followed above, and assign the
next speech to Celia.

[5] *since . . . great show*] There may be a reference here to some topical event, either to
an unidentified inhibition of players, or to the notorious suppression of satirical and li-
centious books, which took place in 1599.

[6] *colour*] kind or nature. Cf. *Lear*, II, ii, 133, where the Quartos read "a fellow of the self-
same *nature*," and the Folio, "a fellow of the self-same *colour*."

[7] *rank . . . smell*] This punning comment on the word "rank," which Touchstone uses in
its sense of "quality" or "place," and Rosalind in that of "rancidity," is precisely paralleled in *Cymb.*, II, i, 15–16: "CLO. Would he had been one of my *rank!* SEC. LORD
[*Aside*]. To have *smelt* like a fool."

you may see the end; for the best is yet to do; and here, where you are, they are coming to perform it.

CEL. Well, the beginning, that is dead and buried.

LE BEAU. There comes an old man and his three sons,—

CEL. I could match this beginning with an old tale.

LE BEAU. Three proper young men, of excellent growth and presence.

ROS. With bills on their necks,[8] "Be it known unto all men by these presents."

LE BEAU. The eldest of the three wrestled with Charles, the Duke's wrestler; which Charles in a moment threw him, and broke three of his ribs, that there is little hope of life in him: so he served the second, and so the third. Yonder they lie; the poor old man, their father, making such pitiful dole over them that all the beholders take his part with weeping.

ROS. Alas!

TOUCH. But what is the sport, monsieur, that the ladies have lost?

LE BEAU. Why, this that I speak of.

TOUCH. Thus men may grow wiser every day: it is the first time that ever I heard breaking of ribs was sport for ladies.

CEL. Or I, I promise thee.

ROS. But is there any else longs to see this broken music[9] in his sides? is there yet another dotes upon rib-breaking? Shall we see this wrestling, cousin?

LE BEAU. You must, if you stay here; for here is the place appointed for the wrestling, and they are ready to perform it.

CEL. Yonder, sure, they are coming: let us now stay and see it.

Flourish. Enter DUKE FREDERICK, LORDS, ORLANDO, CHARLES, *and* Attendants

DUKE F. Come on: since the youth will not be entreated, his own peril on his forwardness.

ROS. Is yonder the man?

LE BEAU. Even he, madam.

CEL. Alas, he is too young! yet he looks successfully.

DUKE F. How now, daughter and cousin! are you crept hither to see the wrestling?

---

[8]*Ros. With bills on their necks*] Thus the Folios. Farmer transferred these words to Le Beau's preceding speech, and interpreted them as meaning "with halberds, or weapons of war, on their shoulders." Lodge in the novel writes of his hero "with his forest *bill on his neck.*" In any case Rosalind puns on the word "bills" [*i.e.* halberds] in the sense of placards or proclamations.

[9]*broken music*] A quibbling use of a technical musical term for a musical performance, in which the instruments employed did not keep tune, according to strict rules of harmony. There is no connection between broken music and broken ribs, save the verbal identity of the epithet.

Ros.   Ay, my liege, so please you give us leave.

Duke F.   You will take little delight in it, I can tell you, there is such odds in the man.[10] In pity of the challenger's youth I would fain dissuade him, but he will not be entreated. Speak to him, ladies; see if you can move him.

Cel.   Call him hither, good Monsieur Le Beau.

Duke F.   Do so: I'll not be by.

Le Beau.   Monsieur the challenger, the princess calls[11] for you.

Orl.   I attend them with all respect and duty.

Ros.   Young man, have you challenged Charles the wrestler?

Orl.   No, fair princess; he is the general challenger: I come but in, as others do, to try with him the strength of my youth.

Cel.   Young gentleman, your spirits are too bold for your years. You have seen cruel proof of this man's strength: if you saw yourself with your eyes, or knew yourself with your judgement,[12] the fear of your adventure would counsel you to a more equal enterprise. We pray you, for your own sake, to embrace your own safety, and give over this attempt.

Ros.   Do, young sir; your reputation shall not therefore be misprised: we will make it our suit to the Duke that the wrestling might not go forward.

Orl.   I beseech you, punish me not with your hard thoughts; wherein I confess me much guilty, to deny so fair and excellent ladies any thing. But let your fair eyes and gentle wishes go with me to my trial: wherein if I be foiled, there is but one shamed that was never gracious; if killed, but one dead that is willing to be so: I shall do my friends no wrong, for I have none to lament me; the world no injury, for in it I have nothing: only in the world I fill up a place, which may be better supplied when I have made it empty.

Ros.   The little strength that I have, I would it were with you.

Cel.   And mine, to eke out hers.

Ros.   Fare you well: pray heaven I be deceived in you!

Cel.   Your heart's desires be with you!

Cha.   Come, where is this young gallant that is so desirous to lie with his mother earth?

Orl.   Ready, sir; but his will hath in it a more modest working.

Duke F.   You shall try but one fall.

Cha.   No, I warrant your Grace, you shall not entreat him to a second, that have so mightily persuaded him from a first.

---

[10]*odds in the man*] advantage on the side of the wrestler Charles.

[11]*princess calls*] Theobald reads *princesses call*, which Orlando's reference to *them* seems to justify.

[12]*saw . . . judgement*] exerted all your powers of vision and judgment.

ORL.   You mean to mock me after; you should not have mocked me
    before: but come your ways.
ROS.   Now Hercules be thy speed, young man!
CEL.   I would I were invisible, to catch the strong fellow by the leg.
                                                    [*They wrestle.*
ROS.   O excellent young man!
CEL.   If I had a thunderbolt in mine eye, I can tell who should down.
                                       [*Shout. Charles is thrown.*
DUKE F.   No more, no more.
ORL.   Yes, I beseech your Grace: I am not yet well breathed.[13]
DUKE F.   How dost thou, Charles?
LE BEAU.   He cannot speak, my lord.
DUKE F.   Bear him away. What is thy name, young man?
ORL.   Orlando, my liege; the youngest son of Sir Rowland de Boys.
DUKE F.   I would thou hadst been son to some man else:
    The world esteem'd thy father honourable,
    But I did find him still mine enemy:
    Thou shouldst have better pleased me with this deed,
    Hadst thou descended from another house.
    But fare thee well; thou art a gallant youth:
    I would thou hadst told me of another father.
                         [*Exeunt* DUKE FRED., *train, and* LE BEAU.
CEL.   Were I my father, coz, would I do this?
ORL.   I am more proud to be Sir Rowland's son,
    His youngest son; and would not change that calling,[14]
    To be adopted heir to Frederick.
ROS.   My father loved Sir Rowland as his soul,
    And all the world was of my father's mind:
    Had I before known this young man his son,
    I should have given him tears unto entreaties,[15]
    Ere he should thus have ventured.
CEL.   Gentle cousin,
    Let us go thank him and encourage him:
    My father's rough and envious disposition
    Sticks me at heart. Sir, you have well deserved:
    If you do keep your promises in love
    But justly, as you have exceeded all promise,
    Your mistress shall be happy.

---

[13]*not yet well breathed*] not yet in thorough practice, in full career. Cf. *Ant. and Cleop.*,
   III, xiii, 178: "I will be treble-sinewed, hearted, *breathed*."
[14]*calling*] name, or appellation. This usage is rare. The word is more common in
   Shakespeare in the modern sense of "vocation" or "profession," especially of an ec-
   clesiastical kind.
[15]*tears unto entreaties*] tears in addition to entreaties.

ROS.   Gentleman,
                       [*Giving him a chain from her neck.*
    Wear this for me, one out of suits with fortune,[16]
    That could give more, but that her hand lacks means.
    Shall we go, coz?
CEL.   Ay. Fare you well, fair gentleman.
ORL.   Can I not say, I thank you? My better parts
    Are all thrown down, and that which here stands up
    Is but a quintain, a mere lifeless block.
ROS.   He calls us back: my pride fell with my fortunes;
    I'll ask him what he would. Did you call, sir?
    Sir, you have wrestled well and overthrown
    More than your enemies.
CEL.   Will you go, coz?
ROS.   Have with you. Fare you well.   [*Exeunt* ROSALIND *and* CELIA.
ORL.   What passion hangs these weights upon my tongue?
    I cannot speak to her, yet she urged conference.
    O poor Orlando, thou art overthrown!
    Or Charles or something weaker masters thee.

Re-enter LE BEAU

LE BEAU.   Good sir, I do in friendship counsel you
    To leave this place. Albeit you have deserved
    High commendation, true applause, and love,
    Yet such is now the Duke's condition,[17]
    That he misconstrues all that you have done.
    The Duke is humorous: what he is, indeed,
    More suits you to conceive than I to speak of.
ORL.   I thank you, sir: and, pray you, tell me this,
    Which of the two was daughter of the Duke,
    That here was at the wrestling?
LE BEAU.   Neither his daughter, if we judge by manners;
    But yet, indeed, the taller[18] is his daughter:
    The other is daughter to the banish'd Duke,
    And here detain'd by her usurping uncle,

---

[16]*out of suits with fortune*] out of fortune's service, deprived of her livery. Cf. I, iii, 24, *infra*: "turning these jests *out of service*."

[17]*condition*] temperament. Cf. *Merch. of Ven.*, I, ii, 143: "the condition [*i.e.* temperament or disposition] of a saint."

[18]*taller*] This is the reading of the Folios. Rowe and almost all subsequent editors read here *shorter* (or *smaller*). A change of the kind seems necessary. Rosalind, in the next scene, line 110, gives as a reason for her assuming a man's disguise when fleeing with Celia that she is "more than common tall," and at IV, iii, 86–87, Celia is described as "low and browner" than Rosalind.

To keep his daughter company; whose loves
Are dearer than the natural bond of sisters.
But I can tell you that of late this Duke
Hath ta'en displeasure 'gainst his gentle niece,
Grounded upon no other argument
But that the people praise her for her virtues,
And pity her for her good father's sake;
And, on my life, his malice 'gainst the lady
Will suddenly break forth. Sir, fare you well.
Hereafter, in a better world than this,
I shall desire more love and knowledge of you.

ORL.   I rest much bounden to you: fare you well.   [*Exit* LE BEAU.
Thus must I from the smoke into the smother;[19]
From tyrant Duke unto a tyrant brother:
But heavenly Rosalind!   [*Exit.*

SCENE III. *A Room in the Palace.*

Enter CELIA *and* ROSALIND

CEL.   Why, cousin! why, Rosalind! Cupid have mercy! not a word?
ROS.   Not one to throw at a dog.
CEL.   No, thy words are too precious to be cast away upon curs; throw
        some of them at me; come, lame me with reasons.
ROS.   Then there were two cousins laid up; when the one should be
        lamed with reasons and the other mad without any.
CEL.   But is all this for your father?
ROS.   No, some of it is for my child's father.[1] O, how full of briers is
        this working-day world!
CEL.   They are but burs, cousin, thrown upon thee in holiday foolery: if
        we walk not in the trodden paths, our very petticoats will catch them.
ROS.   I could shake them off my coat: these burs are in my heart.
CEL.   Hem[2] them away.

---

[19]*from the smoke . . . smother*] from bad to worse. "Smother" is the thick stifling smoke
of a smouldering fire.

[1]*my child's father*] this would mean "my husband." Thus the Folios. Numerous modern
editors substitute *my father's child, i.e.* myself.

[2]*Hem*] an onomatopœic word implying the act of coughing slightly. "Hem them away"
is remove them by a small effort of the throat.

Ros. I would try, if I could cry hem and have him.[3]

Cel. Come, come, wrestle with thy affections.

Ros. O, they take the part of a better wrestler than myself!

Cel. O, a good wish upon you! you will try in time, in despite of a fall. But, turning these jests out of service, let us talk in good earnest: is it possible, on such a sudden, you should fall into so strong a liking with old Sir Rowland's youngest son?

Ros. The Duke my father loved his father dearly.

Cel. Doth it therefore ensue that you should love his son dearly? By this kind of chase, I should hate him, for my father hated his father dearly;[4] yet I hate not Orlando.

Ros. No, faith, hate him not, for my sake.

Cel. Why should I not? doth he not deserve well?

Ros. Let me love him for that, and do you love him because I do. Look, here comes the Duke.

Cel. With his eyes full of anger.

Enter Duke Frederick, *with* Lords

Duke F.   Mistress, dispatch you with your safest[5] haste
And get you from our court.

Ros.   Me, uncle?

Duke F.   You, cousin:
Within these ten days if that thou be'st found
So near our public court as twenty miles,
Thou diest for it.

Ros.   I do beseech your Grace,
Let me the knowledge of my fault bear with me:
If with myself I hold intelligence,
Or have acquaintance with mine own desires;
If that I do not dream, or be not frantic,—
As I do trust I am not,—then, dear uncle,
Never so much as in a thought unborn
Did I offend your Highness.

Duke F.   Thus do all traitors:
If their purgation did consist in words,
They are as innocent as grace itself:
Let it suffice thee that I trust thee not.

Ros. Yet your mistrust cannot make me a traitor:
Tell me whereon the likelihood depends.

Duke F. Thou art thy father's daughter; there's enough.

---

[3] *cry hem and have him*] have for the asking; a proverbial expression.

[4] *dearly*] greatly, extremely. Cf. *Hamlet*, I, ii, 182: "my *dearest* foe."

[5] *safest*] surest, least exposed to doubt or delay.

Ros.   So was I when your Highness took his dukedom;
So was I when your Highness banish'd him:
Treason is not inherited, my lord;
Or, if we did derive it from our friends,
What's that to me? my father was no traitor:
Then, good my liege, mistake me not so much
To think my poverty is treacherous.

CEL.   Dear sovereign, hear me speak.

DUKE F.   Ay, Celia; we stay'd her for your sake,
Else had she with her father ranged along.

CEL.   I did not then entreat to have her stay;
It was your pleasure and your own remorse:
I was too young that time to value her;
But now I know her: if she be a traitor,
Why so am I; we still have slept together,
Rose at an instant, learn'd, play'd, eat together,
And wheresoe'er we went, like Juno's swans,[6]
Still we went coupled and inseparable.

DUKE F.   She is too subtle for thee; and her smoothness,
Her very silence and her patience
Speak to the people, and they pity her.
Thou art a fool: she robs thee of thy name;
And thou wilt show more bright and seem more virtuous
When she is gone. Then open not thy lips:
Firm and irrevocable is my doom
Which I have pass'd upon her; she is banish'd.

CEL.   Pronounce that sentence then on me, my liege:
I cannot live out of her company.

DUKE F.   You are a fool. You, niece, provide yourself:
If you outstay the time, upon mine honour,
And in the greatness of my word, you die.

[*Exeunt* DUKE FREDERICK *and* Lords.

CEL.   O my poor Rosalind, whither wilt thou go?
Wilt thou change fathers? I will give thee mine.
I charge thee, be not thou more grieved than I am.

Ros.   I have more cause.

CEL.   Thou hast not, cousin;
Prithee, be cheerful: know'st thou not, the Duke
Hath banish'd me, his daughter?

---

[6]*like Juno's swans*] There is nothing in classical mythology to justify this simile, which seems due to an error of memory. Ovid associates *Venus* and *not Juno* with swans. Cf. *Met.,* X, 708 *seq.* Shakespeare mentions "Venus' doves" seven times in the course of his works, but he ignores her swans.

ROS.   That he hath not.
CEL.   No, hath not? Rosalind lacks then the love
      Which teacheth thee that thou and I am one:
      Shall we be sunder'd? shall we part, sweet girl?
      No: let my father seek another heir.
      Therefore devise with me how we may fly,
      Whither to go and what to bear with us;
      And do not seek to take your change[7] upon you,
      To bear your griefs yourself and leave me out;
      For, by this heaven, now at our sorrows pale,
      Say what thou canst, I'll go along with thee.
ROS.   Why, whither shall we go?
CEL.   To seek my uncle in the forest of Arden.
ROS.   Alas, what danger will it be to us,
      Maids as we are, to travel forth so far!
      Beauty provoketh thieves sooner than gold.
CEL.   I'll put myself in poor and mean attire
      And with a kind of umber smirch my face;
      The like do you: so shall we pass along
      And never stir assailants.
ROS.   Were it not better,
      Because that I am more than common tall,
      That I did suit me all points like a man?
      A gallant curtle-axe upon my thigh,
      A boar-spear in my hand; and—in my heart
      Lie there what hidden woman's fear there will—
      We'll have a swashing and a martial outside,
      As many other mannish cowards have
      That do outface it with their semblances.
CEL.   What shall I call thee when thou art a man?
ROS.   I'll have no worse a name than Jove's own page;
      And therefore look you call me Ganymede.
      But what will you be call'd?
CEL.   Something that hath a reference to my state;
      No longer Celia, but Aliena.
ROS.   But, cousin, what if we assay'd to steal
      The clownish fool out of your father's court?
      Would he not be a comfort to our travel?
CEL.   He'll go along o'er the wide world with me;
      Leave me alone to woo him. Let's away,

---

[7]*your change*] For this reading of the First Folio the Second and later Folios substituted *your charge*, which seems to improve the sense. But the original reading *change*, *i.e.* "reverse of fortune," may be right.

And get our jewels and our wealth together;
Devise the fittest time and safest way
To hide us from pursuit that will be made
After my flight. Now go we in content
To liberty and not to banishment.   [*Exeunt.*

ACT II.

SCENE I. *The Forest of Arden.*

Enter DUKE SENIOR, AMIENS, *and two or three* Lords, *like foresters*

DUKE S.   Now, my co-mates and brothers in exile,
　　　　Hath not old custom made this life more sweet
　　　　Than that of painted pomp? Are not these woods
　　　　More free from peril than the envious court?
　　　　Here feel we but the penalty of Adam,
　　　　The seasons' difference; as the icy fang
　　　　And churlish chiding of the winter's wind,
　　　　Which, when it bites and blows upon my body,
　　　　Even till I shrink with cold, I smile and say
　　　　"This is no flattery: these are counsellors
　　　　That feelingly persuade me what I am."
　　　　Sweet are the uses of adversity;
　　　　Which, like the toad, ugly and venomous,
　　　　Wears yet a precious jewel in his head:[1]
　　　　And this our life exempt from public haunt
　　　　Finds tongues in trees, books in the running brooks,
　　　　Sermons in stones and good in every thing.
　　　　I would not change it.

AMI.　　　　　　　　　Happy is your Grace,

---

[1] *precious jewel in his head*] Cf. Lyly's *Euphues*: "The foule Toade hath a faire stone in his head" (ed. Arber, p. 53). The ignorant popular belief, that a toad carried a precious stone in its head, which was universal in Shakespeare's day, is apparently derived from the fact that a stone or gem, chiefly found in Egypt, is of the brownish gray colour of toads, and is therefore called a batrachite or toadstone. Pliny in his *Natural History* (Book 32) ascribes to a bone in the toad's head curative and other properties, but does not suggest that a gem is ever found there. In his description elsewhere of the toad-stones of Egypt he only notes their association with toads in the way of colour.

17

That can translate the stubbornness of fortune
Into so quiet and so sweet a style.
DUKE S.   Come, shall we go and kill us venison?
And yet it irks me the poor dappled fools,
Being native burghers of this desert city,
Should in their own confines with forked heads[2]
Have their round haunches gored.
FIRST LORD.   Indeed, my lord,
The melancholy Jaques grieves at that,
And, in that kind, swears you do more usurp
Than doth your brother that hath banish'd you.
To-day my Lord of Amiens and myself
Did steal behind him as he lay along
Under an oak whose antique root peeps out
Upon the brook that brawls along this wood:
To the which place a poor sequester'd stag,
That from the hunter's aim had ta'en a hurt,
Did come to languish, and indeed, my lord,
The wretched animal heaved forth such groans,
That their discharge did stretch his leathern coat
Almost to bursting, and the big round tears
Coursed one another down his innocent nose
In piteous chase; and thus the hairy fool,
Much marked of the melancholy Jaques,
Stood on the extremest verge of the swift brook,
Augmenting it with tears.
DUKE S.   But what said Jaques?
Did he not moralize[3] this spectacle?
FIRST LORD.   O, yes, into a thousand similes.
First, for his weeping into the needless stream;
"Poor deer," quoth he, "thou makest a testament
As worldlings do, giving thy sum of more
To that which had too much": then, being there alone,
Left and abandon'd of his velvet friends;
"'T is right," quoth he; "thus misery doth part
The flux of company": anon a careless herd,
Full of the pasture, jumps along by him
And never stays to greet him; "Ay," quoth Jaques,

---

[2]*forked heads*] arrow heads. Roger Ascham, in *Toxophilus* (ed. Arber, p. 135), mentions that arrow heads, "having two points stretching forwards," are commonly called "fork heads." Cf. *Lear*, I, i, 143, where the arrow-head is called "the fork."
[3]*moralize*] Cf. Cotgrave, *Fr.-Eng. Dict.*: "Moraliser: To *moralize*, to expound morrally, to give a morall sence vnto." See also *infra*, II, vii, 29: "*moral* on the time."

"Sweep on, you fat and greasy citizens;
'T is just the fashion: wherefore do you look
Upon that poor and broken bankrupt there?"
Thus most invectively he pierceth through
The body of the country, city, court,
Yea, and of this our life; swearing that we
Are mere usurpers, tyrants and what's worse,
To fright the animals and to kill them up[4]
In their assign'd and native dwelling-place.

DUKE S.   And did you leave him in this contemplation?

SEC. LORD.   We did, my lord, weeping and commenting
Upon the sobbing deer.

DUKE S.   Show me the place:
I love to cope[5] him in these sullen fits,
For then he's full of matter.

FIRST LORD.   I'll bring you to him straight.   [*Exeunt.*

SCENE II. *A Room in the Palace.*

Enter DUKE FREDERICK, *with* LORDS

DUKE F.   Can it be possible that no man saw them?
It cannot be: some villains of my court
Are of consent and sufferance in this.

FIRST LORD.   I cannot hear of any that did see her.
The ladies, her attendants of her chamber,
Saw her a-bed, and in the morning early
They found the bed untreasured of their mistress.

SEC. LORD.   My lord, the roynish[1] clown, at whom so oft
Your Grace was wont to laugh, is also missing.
Hisperia, the princess' gentlewoman,
Confesses that she secretly o'erheard

---

[4]*kill . . . up*] Intensitive of "kill," *i.e.* exterminate. Cf. Adlington's *Apuleius' Golden Asse*, 1582, fo. 159: "*Killed up* with colde."

[5]*cope*] meet with, encounter. Cf. *Venus and Adonis*, 889: "They all strain courtesy who shall *cope* him first."

---

[1]*roynish*] scurvy. Cognate forms "roynous" and "roignous," both meaning "coarse," figure in the *Romaunt of the Rose*, ll. 987, 6193. The word seems adapted from the French. Cotgrave's *Fr.-Eng. Dict.* has "rougneux," which is interpreted "scabbie, mangie," and "scuruie." Cf. *Macb.*, I, iii, 6: "*rump-fed ronyon* [mangy creature]."

Your daughter and her cousin much commend
The parts and graces of the wrestler
That did but lately foil the sinewy Charles;
And she believes, wherever they are gone,
That youth is surely in their company.

DUKE F.   Send to his brother; fetch that gallant hither;
If he be absent, bring his brother to me;
I'll make him find him: do this suddenly,
And let not search and inquisition quail[2]
To bring again these foolish runaways.   [*Exeunt.*

SCENE III. *Before Oliver's House.*

Enter ORLANDO *and* ADAM, *meeting*

ORL.   Who's there?

ADAM.   What, my young master? O my gentle master!
O my sweet master! O you memory
Of old Sir Rowland! why, what make you here?
Why are you virtuous? why do people love you?
And wherefore are you gentle, strong and valiant?
Why would you be so fond to overcome
The bonny priser[1] of the humorous Duke?
Your praise is come too swiftly home before you.
Know you not, master, to some kind of men
Their graces serve them but as enemies?
No more do yours: your virtues, gentle master,
Are sanctified and holy traitors to you.
O, what a world is this, when what is comely
Envenoms him that bears it!

ORL.   Why, what's the matter?

ADAM.   O unhappy youth!
Come not within these doors; within this roof
The enemy of all your graces lives:

---

[2]*quail*] grow faint, slacken in effort.

[1]*bonny priser*] strong prizefighter (*i.e.*, contender for a prize). The word *bonny* is the reading of all the Folios, and is doubtless right. The epithet is frequently used in the sense of "strong" as well as in that of "comely." Warburton's widely adopted correction, *boney, i.e.*, "muscular," is unnecessary.

Your brother—no, no brother; yet the son—
Yet not the son, I will not call him son,
Of him I was about to call his father,—
Hath heard your praises, and this night he means
To burn the lodging where you use to lie
And you within it: if he fail of that,
He will have other means to cut you off.
I overheard him and his practices.
This is no place;[2] this house is but a butchery:
Abhor it, fear it, do not enter it.

ORL.   Why, whither, Adam, wouldst thou have me go?
ADAM.   No matter whither, so you come not here.
ORL.   What, wouldst thou have me go and beg my food?
Or with a base and boisterous sword enforce
A thievish living on the common road?
This I must do, or know not what to do:
Yet this I will not do, do how I can;
I rather will subject me to the malice
Of a diverted blood[3] and bloody brother.

ADAM.   But do not so. I have five hundred crowns,
The thrifty hire I saved under your father,
Which I did store to be my foster-nurse
When service should in my old limbs lie lame,
And unregarded age in corners thrown:
Take that, and He that doth the ravens feed,
Yea, providently caters for the sparrow,
Be comfort to my age! Here is the gold;
All this I give you. Let me be your servant:
Though I look old, yet I am strong and lusty;
For in my youth I never did apply
Hot and rebellious liquors in my blood,
Nor did not with unbashful forehead woo
The means of weakness and debility;
Therefore my age is as a lusty winter,
Frosty, but kindly: let me go with you;
I'll do the service of a younger man
In all your business and necessities.

ORL.   O good old man, how well in thee appears
The constant service of the antique world,
When service sweat for duty, not for meed!

---

[2]*This is no place*] Cf. *Lover's Complaint*, 82: "Love made him her *place*, [*i.e.*, her home,
  place to dwell in]."
[3]*diverted blood*] blood (or natural affection) turned from the course of nature.

Thou art not for the fashion of these times,
Where none will sweat but for promotion,
And having that do choke their service up
Even with the having: it is not so with thee.
But, poor old man, thou prunest a rotten tree,
That cannot so much as a blossom yield
In lieu of all thy pains and husbandry.
But come thy ways; we'll go along together,
And ere we have thy youthful wages spent,
We'll light upon some settled low content.
ADAM.   Master, go on, and I will follow thee,
To the last gasp, with truth and loyalty.
From seventeen[4] years till now almost fourscore
Here lived I, but now live here no more.
At seventeen years many their fortunes seek;
But at fourscore it is too late a week:
Yet fortune cannot recompense me better
Than to die well and not my master's debtor.   [*Exeunt.*

SCENE IV. *The Forest of Arden.*

Enter ROSALIND *for* GANYMEDE, CELIA *for* ALIENA, *and* TOUCHSTONE

ROS.   O Jupiter, how weary[1] are my spirits!
TOUCH.   I care not for my spirits, if my legs were not weary.
ROS.   I could find in my heart to disgrace my man's apparel and to cry
     like a woman; but I must comfort the weaker vessel, as doublet
     and hose[2] ought to show itself courageous to petticoat: therefore,
     courage, good Aliena.
CEL.   I pray you, bear with me; I cannot go no further.
TOUCH.   For my part, I had rather bear with you than bear you: yet I
     should bear no cross,[3] if I did bear you; for I think you have no
     money in your purse.

---

[4]*seventeen*] This is Rowe's emendation for the *seventy* of the Folios.

[1]*weary*] Theobald's emendation of the *merry* of the Folios.
[2]*doublet and hose*] the chief features of male attire in Shakespeare's day.
[3]*bear no cross*] a quibble on the two meanings of the phrase, viz., "endure hardship" and
     "carry a coin," specifically known as a "cross," from the stamp upon it of a cross. Cf. *2
     Hen. IV*, I, ii, 212–213: "you are too impatient to *bear crosses.*"

Ros.   Well, this is the forest of Arden.

Touch.   Ay, now am I in Arden; the more fool I; when I was at home,
I was in a better place: but travellers must be content.

Ros.   Ay, be so, good Touchstone.

Enter Corin *and* Silvius

Look you, who comes here; a young man and an old in solemn talk.

Cor.   That is the way to make her scorn you still.

Sil.   O Corin, that thou knew'st how I do love her!

Cor.   I partly guess; for I have loved ere now.

Sil.   No, Corin, being old, thou canst not guess,
Though in thy youth thou wast as true a lover
As ever sigh'd upon a midnight pillow:
But if thy love were ever like to mine,—
As sure I think did never man love so,—
How many actions most ridiculous
Hast thou been drawn to by thy fantasy?[+]

Cor.   Into a thousand that I have forgotten.

Sil.   O, thou didst then ne'er love so heartily!
If thou remember'st not the slightest folly
That ever love did make thee run into,
Thou hast not loved:
Or if thou hast not sat as I do now,
Wearing thy hearer in thy mistress' praise,
Thou hast not loved:
Or if thou hast not broke from company
Abruptly, as my passion now makes me,
Thou hast not loved.
O Phebe, Phebe, Phebe!   [*Exit.*

Ros.   Alas, poor shepherd! searching of thy wound, I have by hard adventure found mine own.

Touch.   And I mine. I remember, when I was in love I broke my
sword upon a stone and bid him take that for coming a-night to
Jane Smile: and I remember the kissing of her batlet[5] and the
cow's dugs that her pretty chopt[6] hands had milked: and I remember the wooing of a peascod instead of her; from whom I took
two cods and, giving her them again, said with weeping tears

[+]*fantasy*] Used like the cognate form "fancy" in the sense of affection or love.
[5]*batlet*] Thus the Second and later Folios. The First Folio reads *batler*, which there seems
no reason for changing. Neither form is met elsewhere. The reference is to the bat or flat
wooden instrument (sometimes called a washing-beetle) with which clothes are beaten
by the laundress. Cf. Levins's *Manipulus*, 1570, p. 38: "To *battle* clothes. Excutere."
[6]*chopt*] chapped. Cf. *Sonnet* lxii, 10: "*chopp'd* with tann'd antiquity."

"Wear these for my sake." We that are true lovers run into strange
capers; but as all is mortal in nature, so is all nature in love mortal in folly.[7]

ROS.   Thou speakest wiser than thou art ware of.

TOUCH.   Nay, I shall ne'er be ware of mine own wit till I break my
shins against it.

ROS.   Jove, Jove! this shepherd's passion
Is much upon my fashion.

TOUCH.   And mine; but it grows something stale with me.

CEL.   I pray you, one of you question yond man
If he for gold will give us any food:
I faint almost to death.

TOUCH.   Holla, you clown!

ROS.   Peace, fool: he's not thy kinsman.

COR.   Who calls?

TOUCH.   Your betters, sir.

COR.   Else are they very wretched.

ROS.   Peace, I say. Good even to you, friend.

COR.   And to you, gentle sir, and to you all.

ROS.   I prithee, shepherd, if that love or gold
Can in this desert place buy entertainment,
Bring us where we may rest ourselves and feed:
Here's a young maid with travel much oppress'd
And faints for succour.

COR.   Fair sir, I pity her
And wish, for her sake more than for mine own,
My fortunes were more able to relieve her;
But I am shepherd to another man
And do not shear the fleeces that I graze:
My master is of churlish disposition
And little recks to find the way to heaven
By doing deeds of hospitality:
Besides, his cote, his flocks and bounds of feed
Are now on sale, and at our sheepcote now,
By reason of his absence, there is nothing
That you will feed on; but what is, come see,
And in my voice[8] most welcome shall you be.

ROS.   What is he that shall buy his flock and pasture?

COR.   That young swain that you saw here but erewhile,
That little cares for buying any thing.

ROS.   I pray thee, if it stand with honesty,

---

[7] *mortal in folly*] "Mortal" is here a slang intensitive meaning "excessive," "extravagant,"
with the implied suggestion that folly deals death to love.

[8] *in my voice*] as far as my voice or vote has power to bid you welcome.

Buy thou the cottage, pasture and the flock,
And thou shalt have to pay for it of us.

CEL.   And we will mend thy wages. I like this place,
And willingly could waste my time in it.

COR.   Assuredly the thing is to be sold:
Go with me: if you like upon report
The soil, the profit and this kind of life,
I will your very faithful feeder[9] be
And buy it with your gold right suddenly.   [*Exeunt.*

SCENE V. *The Forest.*

Enter AMIENS, JAQUES, *and others*

SONG

AMI.

Under the greenwood tree
Who loves to lie with me,
And turn[1] his merry note
Unto the sweet bird's throat,
Come hither, come hither, come hither:
Here shall he see
No enemy
But winter and rough weather.

JAQ.   More, more, I prithee, more.

AMI.   It will make you melancholy, Monsieur Jaques.

JAQ.   I thank it. More, I prithee, more. I can suck melancholy out of
a song, as a weasel sucks eggs. More, I prithee, more.

AMI.   My voice is ragged: I know I cannot please you.

JAQ.   I do not desire you to please me; I do desire you to sing. Come,
more; another stanzo:[2] call you 'em stanzos?

AMI.   What you will, Monsieur Jaques.

---

[9]*feeder*] This word in the sense of "servant" is not uncommon, and various suggested
changes are unnecessary.

[1]*turn*] This is the reading of the Folios, and the word clearly means "adapt." Cf. Hall's
Satires, VI, i: "Martiall *turns* his merry note." Rowe's widely accepted emendation,
tunes, may be rejected.

[2]*stanzo*] Cotgrave, *Fr.-Eng. Dict.*, gives the form "stanzo" (for stanza) when interpret-
ing the French "stance." In *L. L. L.*, IV, ii, 99, "stanze" is read in the original editions,—the First Folio and First Quarto,—and "stanza" in the later Folios. There is an
obvious uncertainty as to the right form.

JAQ. Nay, I care not for their names; they owe me nothing.[3] Will you
       sing?

AMI. More at your request than to please myself.

JAQ. Well then, if ever I thank any man, I'll thank you; but that they
       call compliment is like the encounter of two dog-apes, and when
       a man thanks me heartily, methinks I have given him a penny and
       he renders me the beggarly thanks. Come, sing; and you that will
       not, hold your tongues.

AMI. Well, I'll end the song. Sirs, cover[4] the while; the Duke will
       drink under this tree. He hath been all this day to look you.

JAQ. And I have been all this day to avoid him. He is too disputable
       for my company: I think of as many matters as he; but I give
       heaven thanks, and make no boast of them. Come, warble, come.

SONG

Who doth ambition shun,   [*All together here.*
And loves to live i' the sun,
Seeking the food he eats,
And pleased with what he gets,
Come hither, come hither, come hither:
Here shall he see
No enemy
But winter and rough weather.

JAQ. I'll give you a verse to this note, that I made yesterday in despite
       of my invention.

AMI. And I'll sing it.

JAQ. Thus it goes: —

If it do come to pass
That any man turn ass,
Leaving his wealth and ease
A stubborn will to please,
Ducdame, ducdame, ducdame:[5]
Here shall he see
Gross fools as he,
And if he will come to me.

---

[3]*names . . . owe me nothing*] an allusion to the use of the Latin "nomina" in the common sense of "details of debt." Cooper's *Thesaurus*, 1573, defines "Nomina" as "the
names of debtes owen."

[4]*cover*] lay the cloth.

[5]*Ducdame*] In all probability a nonsensical parody of the conventional burden of an
unidentified popular song. Cf. in *All's Well*, I, iii, 69, the clown's senseless sing-song
"Fond done, done fond" in his ditty of Helen of Greece. Attempts have been made to
connect "ducdame" with like-sounding words in Latin, Italian, French, Gaelic, Welsh,
Greek, and Romany.

AMI.   What's that "ducdame"?

JAQ.   'T is a Greek invocation, to call fools into a circle. I'll go sleep, if I can; if I cannot, I'll rail against all the first-born of Egypt.[6]

AMI.   And I'll go seek the Duke: his banquet is prepared.

                                        [*Exeunt severally.*

SCENE VI. *The Forest.*

Enter ORLANDO *and* ADAM

ADAM.   Dear master, I can go no further; O, I die for food! Here lie I down, and measure out my grave. Farewell, kind master.

ORL.   Why, how now, Adam! no greater heart in thee? Live a little; comfort a little; cheer thyself a little. If this uncouth forest yield any thing savage, I will either be food for it or bring it for food to thee. Thy conceit is nearer death than thy powers. For my sake be comfortable; hold death awhile at the arm's end: I will here be with thee presently; and if I bring thee not something to eat, I will give thee leave to die: but if thou diest before I come, thou art a mocker of my labour. Well said! thou lookest cheerly, and I'll be with thee quickly. Yet thou liest in the bleak air: come, I will bear thee to some shelter; and thou shalt not die for lack of a dinner, if there live any thing in this desert. Cheerly, good Adam!   [*Exeunt.*

SCENE VII. *The Forest.*

A table set out. Enter DUKE SENIOR, AMIENS, *and* Lords *like outlaws*

DUKE S.   I think he be transform'd into a beast;
     For I can no where find him like a man.

FIRST LORD.   My lord, he is but even now gone hence:
     Here was he merry, hearing of a song.

[6]*the first-born of Egypt*] high-born persons.

DUKE S.   If he, compact of jars, grow musical,
    We shall have shortly discord in the spheres.[1]
    Go, seek him: tell him I would speak with him.

Enter JAQUES

FIRST LORD.   He saves my labour by his own approach.
DUKE S.   Why, how now, monsieur! what a life is this,
    That your poor friends must woo your company?
    What, you look merrily!
JAQ.   A fool, a fool! I met a fool i' the forest,
    A motley[2] fool; a miserable world!
    As I do live by food, I met a fool;
    Who laid him down and bask'd him in the sun,
    And rail'd on Lady Fortune in good terms,
    In good set terms, and yet a motley fool.
    "Good morrow, fool," quoth I. "No, sir," quoth he,
    "Call me not fool till heaven hath sent me fortune:"
    And then he drew a dial from his poke,[3]
    And, looking on it with lack-lustre eye,
    Says very wisely, "It is ten o'clock:
    Thus we may see," quoth he, "how the world wags:
    'T is but an hour ago since it was nine;
    And after one hour more 't will be eleven;
    And so, from hour to hour, we ripe and ripe,
    And then, from hour to hour, we rot and rot;
    And thereby hangs a tale." When I did hear
    The motley fool thus moral[4] on the time,
    My lungs began to crow like chanticleer,
    That fools should be so deep-contemplative;
    And I did laugh sans intermission

[1]*spheres*] The common belief in the music of the spheres is well illustrated in *Merch. of Ven.*, V, i, 60–61: "There's not the smallest orb which thou behold'st But in his motion like an angel sings."

[2]*motley*] a reference to the conventional parti-coloured or patchwork dress of the professional fool. "Mottled" would be the modern expression. A species of variegated cloth seems to have borne in the trade the name of "motley." Cf. line 34, *infra*, "*Motley's* the only wear," and 43, "a *motley* coat."

[3]*dial from his poke*] It was common among the lower orders to carry in the "poke" or pocket a sundial in the form of a metal ring about two inches in diameter, which was so marked and contrived that sunlight falling upon it indicated the hour of day. A specimen of a pocket dial of the Elizabethan period is preserved in the Museum at Shakespeare's birthplace, Stratford-upon-Avon.

[4]*moral*] Cf. II, i, 44, *supra*, "*moralize* this spectacle." There seems little doubt that "moral on" is a verb meaning "moralize on." The suggestion that "moral" is here used adjectivally offers an awkward construction.

       An hour by his dial. O noble fool!
       A worthy fool! Motley's the only wear.
DUKE S.   What fool is this?
JAQ.   O worthy fool! One that hath been a courtier,
       And says, if ladies be but young and fair,
       They have the gift to know it: and in his brain,
       Which is as dry as the remainder biscuit
       After a voyage, he hath strange places cramm'd[5]
       With observation, the which he vents
       In mangled forms. O that I were a fool!
       I am ambitious for a motley coat.
DUKE S.   Thou shalt have one.
JAQ.   It is my only suit;[6]
       Provided that you weed your better judgements
       Of all opinion that grows rank in them
       That I am wise. I must have liberty
       Withal, as large a charter as the wind,[7]
       To blow on whom I please; for so fools have;
       And they that are most galled with my folly,
       They most must laugh. And why, sir, must they so?
       The "why" is plain as way to parish church:
       He that a fool doth very wisely hit
       Doth very foolishly, although he smart,
       Not to seem senseless of the bob:[8] if not,
       The wise man's folly is anatomized
       Even by the squandering glances[9] of the fool.
       Invest me in my motley; give me leave
       To speak my mind, and I will through and through
       Cleanse the foul body of the infected world,
       If they will patiently receive my medicine.
DUKE S.   Fie on thee! I can tell what thou wouldst do.
JAQ.   What, for a counter,[10] would I do but good?
DUKE S.   Most mischievous foul sin, in chiding sin:

---

[5]*he hath strange places cramm'd*] he hath collected from observation or study a mass of
   strange topics, allusions, passages from books. Cf. the use of the Latin word "loci" and
   the Greek "τόποι."
[6]*my only suit*] a quibble on the two meanings of the word "petition" and "dress."
[7]*as large a charter as the wind*] Cf. *Hen. V*, I, i, 48: "The *air*, a *charter'd libertine*, is still."
[8]*Not to . . . bob*] The Folios omit the words *not to*, which Theobald first supplied. They
   are necessary to the sense. The general meaning is that the wise man, though he may
   smart under a fool's taunt, ought to ignore the "bob" or rap of a fool's comment.
[9]*squandering glances*] random shots.
[10]*counter*] a thing of no value; a metal disc, of no intrinsic value, used in making
   calculations.

> For thou thyself hast been a libertine,
> As sensual as the brutish sting[11] itself;
> And all the embossed sores and headed evils,
> That thou with license of free foot[12] hast caught,
> Wouldst thou disgorge into the general world.

JAQ.   Why, who cries out on pride,
>   That can therein tax any private party?
>   Doth it not flow as hugely as the sea,
>   Till that the weary very means do ebb?[13]
>   What woman in the city do I name,
>   When that I say the city-woman bears
>   The cost of princes on unworthy shoulders?
>   Who can come in and say that I mean her,
>   When such a one as she such is her neighbour?
>   Or what is he of basest function,
>   That says his bravery is not on my cost,
>   Thinking that I mean him, but therein suits
>   His folly to the mettle of my speech?[14]
>   There then; how then? what then? Let me see wherein
>   My tongue hath wrong'd him: if it do him right,
>   Then he hath wrong'd himself; if he be free,
>   Why then my taxing like a wild-goose flies,
>   Unclaim'd of any man. But who comes here?

Enter ORLANDO, *with his sword drawn*

ORL.   Forbear, and eat no more.
JAQ.   Why, I have eat none yet.
ORL.   Nor shalt not, till necessity be served.
JAQ.   Of what kind should this cock come of?
DUKE S.   Art thou thus bolden'd, man, by thy distress?
>   Or else a rude despiser of good manners,
>   That in civility thou seem'st so empty?
ORL.   You touch'd my vein at first: the thorny point
>   Of bare distress hath ta'en from me the show

---

[11]*brutish sting*] animal impulse.

[12]*with license of free foot*] gadding about with no restraint.

[13]*Till . . . ebb*] This is the original reading. It means that pride flows on like the tidal sea till its "very means," or sustaining forces, becoming weary or exhausted, ebb or decay. Singer's emendation, *the wearer's very means,* is not happy.

[14]*Or what . . . speech?*] The general meaning is that one finds men in the lowest position in life taking a foolish pride in showy apparel who, if they hear a censorious observer denounce the vanity of spending money on dress, retort that the critic does not pay for what they wear; the critic's censure is intended to have no particular or personal application, but such a reply is a safe sign that the cap fits.

Of smooth civility: yet am I inland[15] bred
And know some nurture. But forbear, I say:
He dies that touches any of this fruit
Till I and my affairs are answered.

JAQ.   An you will not be answered with reason, I must die.

DUKE S.   What would you have? Your gentleness shall force,
More than your force move us to gentleness.

ORL.   I almost die for food; and let me have it.

DUKE S.   Sit down and feed, and welcome to our table.

ORL.   Speak you so gently? Pardon me, I pray you:
I thought that all things had been savage here;
And therefore put I on the countenance
Of stern commandment. But whate'er you are
That in this desert inaccessible,
Under the shade of melancholy boughs,
Lose and neglect the creeping hours of time;
If ever you have look'd on better days,
If ever been where bells have knoll'd to church,
If ever sat at any good man's feast,
If ever from your eyelids wiped a tear
And know what 't is to pity and be pitied,
Let gentleness my strong enforcement be:
In the which hope I blush, and hide my sword.

DUKE S.   True is it that we have seen better days,
And have with holy bell been knoll'd to church,
And sat at good men's feasts, and wiped our eyes
Of drops that sacred pity hath engender'd:
And therefore sit you down in gentleness
And take upon command[16] what help we have
That to your wanting may be minister'd.

ORL.   Then but forbear your food a little while,
Whiles, like a doe, I go to find my fawn
And give it food. There is an old poor man,
Who after me hath many a weary step
Limp'd in pure love: till he be first sufficed,
Oppress'd with two weak evils, age and hunger,
I will not touch a bit.

DUKE S.   Go find him out,
And we will nothing waste till you return.

ORL.   I thank ye; and be blest for your good comfort!   [*Exit.*

---

[15]*inland*] civilized, refined, the converse of "outlandish." Cf. III, ii, 322, *infra:* "an inland man."

[16]*upon command*] at your command.

DUKE S.   Thou seest we are not all alone unhappy:
      This wide and universal theatre
      Presents more woeful pageants than the scene
      Wherein we play in.
JAQ.   All the world's a stage,[17]
      And all the men and women merely players:
      They have their exits and their entrances;
      And one man in his time plays many parts,
      His acts being seven ages. At first the infant,
      Mewling and puking in the nurse's arms.
      Then the whining school-boy, with his satchel
      And shining morning face, creeping like snail
      Unwillingly to school. And then the lover,
      Sighing like furnace,[18] with a woeful ballad
      Made to his mistress' eyebrow. Then a soldier,
      Full of strange oaths, and bearded like the pard,
      Jealous in honour, sudden and quick in quarrel,
      Seeking the bubble reputation
      Even in the cannon's mouth. And then the justice,
      In fair round belly with good capon[19] lined,
      With eyes severe and beard of formal cut,
      Full of wise saws and modern instances;[20]
      And so he plays his part. The sixth age shifts
      Into the lean and slipper'd pantaloon,
      With spectacles on nose and pouch on side,
      His youthful hose, well saved, a world too wide
      For his shrunk shank; and his big manly voice,
      Turning again toward childish treble, pipes
      And whistles in his sound. Last scene of all,
      That ends this strange eventful history,
      Is second childishness and mere oblivion,

[17]*All . . . stage*] Cf. *Merch. of Ven.*, I, i, 77–78: "I hold the world but as the world, Gratiano; A stage, where every man must play a part." The comparison of the world to a stage was a commonplace in Greek, Latin, and modern European literature. The Globe Theatre bore the proverbial motto, "Totus mundus agit histrionem." The division of man's life into seven parts or ages, which Shakespeare likens to acts of a play, is found in the Greek writings of the physician Hippocrates and of the late Greek philosopher Proclus, and was generally accepted by philosophers, poets, and artists of the European Renaissance.

[18]*Sighing like furnace*] Cf. *Cymb.*, I, vi, 65–66: "he [*i.e.*, a Frenchman in love] *furnaces* The thick *sighs* from him."

[19]*the justice . . . capon*] Capons formed gifts which suitors were in the habit of offering justices of the peace. Cf. Wither's *Christmas Carol*, lines 41, 42: "Now poor men to the *justices* With *capons* make their arrants [*i.e.*, errands]."

[20]*modern instances*] trite or commonplace maxims or anecdotes.

Sans teeth, sans eyes, sans taste, sans every thing.

Re-enter ORLANDO, *with* ADAM

DUKE S.   Welcome. Set down your venerable burthen,
    And let him feed.
ORL.   I thank you most for him.
ADAM.   So had you need:
    I scarce can speak to thank you for myself.
DUKE S.   Welcome; fall to: I will not trouble you
    As yet, to question you about your fortunes.
    Give us some music; and, good cousin, sing.

SONG

AMI.   Blow, blow, thou winter wind,
               Thou art not so unkind
                  As man's ingratitude;
               Thy tooth is not so keen,
               Because thou art not seen,
                  Although thy breath be rude.
     Heigh-ho! sing, heigh-ho! unto the green holly:
   Most friendship is feigning, most loving mere folly:
             Then, heigh-ho, the holly!
               This life is most jolly.

            Freeze, freeze, thou bitter sky,
               That does not bite so nigh
                  As benefits forgot:
               Though thou the waters warp,
               Thy sting is not so sharp
                  As friend remember'd not.
             Heigh-ho! sing, &c.

DUKE S.   If that you were the good Sir Rowland's son,
    As you have whisper'd faithfully you were,
    And as mine eye doth his effigies[21] witness
    Most truly limn'd and living in your face,
    Be truly welcome hither: I am the Duke
    That loved your father: the residue of your fortune,
    Go to my cave and tell me. Good old man,
    Thou art right welcome as thy master is.
    Support him by the arm. Give me your hand,
    And let me all your fortunes understand.   [*Exeunt.*

---

[21]*effigies*] The accent in this word, which must be pronounced trisyllabically, falls on
the second syllable.

ACT III.

SCENE I. *A Room in the Palace*.

Enter DUKE FREDERICK, Lords, *and* OLIVER

DUKE FREDERICK.   Not see him since? Sir, sir, that cannot be:
    But were I not the better part made mercy,
    I should not seek an absent argument
    Of my revenge, thou present. But look to it:
    Find out thy brother, wheresoe'er he is;
    Seek him with candle; bring him dead or living
    Within this twelvemonth, or turn thou no more
    To seek a living in our territory:
    Thy lands and all things that thou dost call thine
    Worth seizure do we seize into our hands,
    Till thou canst quit thee by thy brother's mouth
    Of what we think against thee.
OLI.   O that your Highness knew my heart in this!
    I never loved my brother in my life.
DUKE F.   More villain thou. Well, push him out of doors;
    And let my officers of such a nature
    Make an extent upon[1] his house and lands:
    Do this expediently and turn him going.   [*Exeunt*.

---

[1] *Make an extent upon, etc.*] In strict legal phraseology the process of "making an extent," *i.e.*, executing the writ "extendi facias," consisted in appraising the value of property to its full extent as a preliminary to its summary seizure. The process ordinarily followed a sentence of forfeiture of which in the present instance Shakespeare gives no hint. The phrase is very commonly met with in Elizabethan plays in the loose significance, as here, of taking forcible possession of property.

SCENE II. *The Forest.*

Enter ORLANDO, *with a paper*

ORL.   Hang there, my verse, in witness of my love:
      And thou, thrice-crowned queen of night,[1] survey
  With thy chaste eye, from thy pale sphere above,
      Thy huntress' name that my full life doth sway.
  O Rosalind! these trees shall be my books
      And in their barks my thoughts I'll character;
  That every eye which in this forest looks
      Shall see thy virtue witness'd every where.
  Run, run, Orlando; carve on every tree
  The fair, the chaste and unexpressive[2] she.   *[Exit.*

Enter CORIN *and* TOUCHSTONE

COR.   And how like you this shepherd's life, Master Touchstone?
TOUCH.   Truly, shepherd, in respect of itself, it is a good life; but in respect that it is a shepherd's life, it is naught. In respect that it is
solitary, I like it very well; but in respect that it is private, it is a very
vile life. Now, in respect it is in the fields, it pleaseth me well; but
in respect it is not in the court, it is tedious. As it is a spare life, look
you, it fits my humour well; but as there is no more plenty in it, it
goes much against my stomach. Hast any philosophy in thee,
shepherd?
COR.   No more but that I know the more one sickens the worse at ease
he is; and that he that wants money, means and content is without
three good friends; that the property of rain is to wet and fire to
burn; that good pasture makes fat sheep, and that a great cause of
the night is lack of the sun; that he that hath learned no wit by nature nor art may complain of good breeding[3] or comes of a very
dull kindred.

---

[1]*thrice-crowned queen of night*] Luna, or the moon, was believed in classical mythology
to rule three realms,—earth, heaven, where she was known as "Diana," and the infer-
nal regions, where she was known as "Hecate." Chapman, in his *Hymn to Night*
(1594), describes how the goddess with "triple forehead" controls earth, seas, and hell.
Cf. *Mids. N. Dr.*, V, i, 391: "the *triple* Hecate's team."
[2]*unexpressive*] inexpressible; a common usage. Cf. Milton's *Lycidas*, 176: "The *unexpressive* nuptial song."
[3]*good breeding*] i.e., the want of good breeding; a common manner of speech in
Elizabethan English.

TOUCH. Such a one is a natural philosopher. Wast ever in court, shepherd?

COR. No, truly.

TOUCH. Then thou art damned.

COR. Nay, I hope.

TOUCH. Truly, thou art damned, like an ill-roasted egg all on one side.

COR. For not being at court? Your reason.

TOUCH. Why, if thou never wast at court, thou never sawest good manners; if thou never sawest good manners, then thy manners must be wicked; and wickedness is sin, and sin is damnation. Thou art in a parlous state, shepherd.

COR. Not a whit, Touchstone: those that are good manners at the court are as ridiculous in the country as the behaviour of the country is most mockable at the court. You told me you salute not at the court, but you kiss[+] your hands: that courtesy would be uncleanly, if courtiers were shepherds.

TOUCH. Instance, briefly; come, instance.

COR. Why, we are still handling our ewes, and their fells, you know, are greasy.

TOUCH. Why, do not your courtier's hands sweat? and is not the grease of a mutton as wholesome as the sweat of a man? Shallow, shallow. A better instance, I say; come.

COR. Besides, our hands are hard.

TOUCH. Your lips will feel them the sooner. Shallow again. A more sounder instance, come.

COR. And they are often tarred over with the surgery of our sheep; and would you have us kiss tar? The courtier's hands are perfumed with civet.

TOUCH. Most shallow man! thou worms-meat, in respect of a good piece of flesh indeed! Learn of the wise, and perpend: civet is of a baser birth than tar, the very uncleanly flux of a cat. Mend the instance, shepherd.

COR. You have too courtly a wit for me: I'll rest.

TOUCH. Wilt thou rest damned? God help thee, shallow man! God make incision in thee! thou art raw.[5]

COR. Sir, I am a true labourer: I earn that I eat, get that I wear, owe no man hate, envy no man's happiness, glad of other men's good, content with my harm, and the greatest of my pride is to see my ewes graze and my lambs suck.

[+]*but you kiss*] without kissing.
[5]*God make incision . . . raw*] A reference to blood-letting, which was the accepted method of treating diseases alike of mind or body. "Raw" seems used in a double sense of "ignorant" and "suffering from a flesh wound," which requires medical treatment.

Touch.   That is another simple sin in you, to bring the ewes and the
          rams together and to offer to get your living by the copulation of
          cattle; to be bawd to a bell-wether, and to betray a she-lamb of a
          twelvemonth to a crooked-pated, old, cuckoldly ram, out of all
          reasonable match. If thou beest not damned for this, the devil
          himself will have no shepherds; I cannot see else how thou
          shouldst 'scape.
Cor.   Here comes young Master Ganymede, my new mistress's brother.

Enter Rosalind, *with a paper, reading*

Ros.   From the east to western Ind,
                         No jewel is like Rosalind.
                         Her worth, being mounted on the wind,
                         Through all the world bears Rosalind.
                         All the pictures fairest lined
                         Are but black to Rosalind.
                         Let no face be kept in mind
                         But the fair of Rosalind.

Touch.   I'll rhyme you so eight years together, dinners and suppers
          and sleeping-hours excepted: it is the right butter-women's rank[6]
          to market.
Ros.   Out, fool!
Touch.   For a taste:

                         If a hart do lack a hind,
                         Let him seek out Rosalind.
                         If the cat will after kind,
                         So be sure will Rosalind.
                         Winter garments must be lined,
                         So must slender Rosalind.
                         They that reap must sheaf and bind;
                         Then to cart with Rosalind.
                         Sweetest nut hath sourest rind,
                         Such a nut is Rosalind.
                         He that sweetest rose will find,
                         Must find love's prick and Rosalind.

[6]*rank*] This, the original reading, has been much questioned, and the numerous suggested substitutes for *rank* include *rate, rack, canter,* and others. It is clear that the
sense required is that of a jog trot or ambling pace, such as characterises butter-women
on their way to market. Such a meaning may possibly be deducible from the women's
practice of riding or walking in file or *rank*. Cf. Pettie's translation of Guazzo's, *Civil
Conversation* (1586): "All the women in the towne runne thether *of a ranke*, as it were
in procession." But much is to be said for the emendation *rack*, which was in common
use for a horse's jogging method of progression.

This is the very false gallop[7] of verses: why do you infect yourself
with them?

Ros.   Peace, you dull fool! I found them on a tree.

Touch.   Truly, the tree yields bad fruit.

Ros.   I'll graff it with you, and then I shall graff it with a medlar: then
it will be the earliest fruit[8] i' the country; for you'll be rotten ere
you be half ripe, and that's the right virtue of the medlar.

Touch.   You have said; but whether wisely or no, let the forest judge.

Enter CELIA, *with a writing*

Ros.   Peace!
Here comes my sister, reading: stand aside.

CEL. [*reads*]   Why should this a desert be?
                         For it is unpeopled? No;
                    Tongues I'll hang on every tree,
                         That shall civil sayings show:
                    Some, how brief the life of man
                         Runs his erring pilgrimage,
                    That the stretching of a span
                         Buckles in his sum of age;
                    Some, of violated vows
                         'Twixt the souls of friend and friend:
                    But upon the fairest boughs,
                         Or at every sentence end,
                    Will I Rosalinda write,
                         Teaching all that read to know
                    The quintessence of every sprite
                         Heaven would in little[9] show.
                    Therefore Heaven Nature charged
                         That one body should be fill'd
                    With all graces wide-enlarged:
                         Nature presently distill'd
                    Helen's cheek, but not her heart,
                         Cleopatra's majesty,

[7]*false gallop*] Cf. Nashe's *Foure Letters*, "I would trot *a false gallop* through the rest of
his ragged *verses*." The term technically means the jerky amble in which the horse puts
the left foot before the right. Shakespeare, in *1 Hen. IV*, III, i, 134–135, likens "minc-
ing poetry" to the "forced gait of a shuffling nag."

[8]*earliest fruit*] The medlar is now one of the latest fruits to ripen. The circumstance that
it rots ere it ripens argues a premature precocity, which may justify Rosalind's quibbling argument.

[9]*in little*] The train of thought has here astrological significance, and "in little" probably refers to the "microcosm, the little world of man," which is a miniature reflection
of the stars. "A picture *in little*," as in *Hamlet*, II, ii, 362, was a common synonym for
a miniature painting. But there is no such reference here.

> Atalanta's better part,[10]
>> Sad Lucretia's modesty.
> Thus Rosalind of many parts
>> By heavenly synod was devised;
> Of many faces, eyes and hearts,
>> To have the touches dearest prized.
> Heaven would that she these gifts should have,
> And I to live and die her slave.

Ros.   O most gentle pulpiter![11] what tedious homily of love have you
wearied your parishioners withal, and never cried "Have patience,
good people"!

Cel.   How now! back, friends! Shepherd, go off a little. Go with him,
sirrah.

Touch.   Come, shepherd, let us make an honourable retreat; though
not with bag and baggage, yet with scrip and scrippage.

> [*Exeunt* CORIN *and* TOUCHSTONE.

Cel.   Didst thou hear these verses?

Ros.   O, yes, I heard them all, and more too; for some of them had in
them more feet than the verses would bear.

Cel.   That's no matter: the feet might bear the verses.

Ros.   Ay, but the feet were lame and could not bear themselves without the verse and therefore stood lamely in the verse.

Cel.   But didst thou hear without wondering how thy name should be
hanged and carved upon these trees?

Ros.   I was seven of the nine days out of the wonder before you came;
for look here what I found on a palm-tree. I was never so be-
rhymed since Pythagoras' time, that I was an Irish rat,[12] which I
can hardly remember.

Cel.   Trow you who hath done this?

Ros.   Is it a man?

---

[10]*Atalanta's better part*] Ovid declares himself unable to decide whether Atalanta more
excelled in swiftness of foot or in beauty of face (*Met.*, X, 562–563). In line 260, *infra*,
reference is made to "Atalanta's heels," the first of her two distinctive characteristics.
At this place Shakespeare probably had in mind the charm of feature which Ovid puts
to her credit.

[11]*pulpiter*] *i.e.*, preacher. This is Spedding's ingenious substitute for *Jupiter* of the Folios.
But Rosalind has already made one appeal to Jupiter (II, iv, 1), and has twice called
on Jove (II, iv, 56), while she makes a passing reference to the god at III, ii, 221, *infra*.
Irrelevant use of these expletives of adjuration seems in keeping with her character,
and the old reading may possibly be right.

[12]*be-rhymed . . . Irish rat*] Cf. Jonson's *Poetaster*, Dialogue to the Reader, 150–151:
"Rime 'hem to death, as they doe *Irish rats* In drumming tunes." The superstitious belief that rats can be rhymed to death seems to be cherished by the peasantry of France
as well as of Ireland.

CEL. And a chain, that you once wore, about his neck. Change you colour?

ROS. I prithee, who?

CEL. O Lord, Lord! it is a hard matter for friends to meet; but mountains may be removed with earthquakes and so encounter.

ROS. Nay, but who is it?

CEL. Is it possible?

ROS. Nay, I prithee now with most petitionary vehemence, tell me who it is.

CEL. O wonderful, wonderful, and most wonderful wonderful! and yet again wonderful, and after that, out of all hooping![13]

ROS. Good my complexion![14] dost thou think, though I am caparisoned like a man, I have a doublet and hose in my disposition? One inch of delay more is a South-sea of discovery;[15] I prithee, tell me who is it quickly, and speak apace. I would thou couldst stammer, that thou mightst pour this concealed man out of thy mouth, as wine comes out of a narrow-mouthed bottle, either too much at once, or none at all. I prithee, take the cork out of thy mouth that I may drink thy tidings.

CEL. So you may put a man in your belly.

ROS. Is he of God's making?[16] What manner of man? Is his head worth a hat? or his chin worth a beard?

CEL. Nay, he hath but a little beard.

ROS. Why, God will send more, if the man will be thankful: let me stay the growth of his beard, if thou delay me not the knowledge of his chin.

CEL. It is young Orlando, that tripped up the wrestler's heels and your heart both in an instant.

ROS. Nay, but the devil take mocking: speak sad brow and true maid.[17]

CEL. I' faith, coz, 't is he.

---

[13]*out of all hooping!*] beyond all the limits of wonder which shouting can adequately express.

[14]*Good my complexion!*] This exclamation seems a nervous and involuntary appeal to Rosalind's feminine tell-tale complexion. The inversion of the epithet "good," which is very common in Elizabethan English, somewhat obscures the meaning, which amounts in effect to nothing more than an ebullition of anxiety lest her girl's face shall betray her.

[15]*One inch of delay more is a South-sea of discovery*] The slightest delay in satisfying my curiosity will expose me to the uncertainties and perplexities of an exploring voyage in some great unknown ocean like the unexplored South-sea or Pacific Ocean.

[16]*of God's making?*] The implied alternative is "a man of his tailor's making." Cf. *Lear*, II, ii, 50: "nature disclaims in thee: a tailor made thee."

[17]*speak . . . maid*] speak in all seriousness and truth. Cf. for the construction 258, *infra*, "I *answer you right painted cloth*," and *K. John*, II, i, 462: "He *speaks plain cannon fire*, and smoke and bounce."

Ros.   Orlando?

Cel.   Orlando.

Ros.   Alas the day! what shall I do with my doublet and hose? What did he when thou sawest him? What said he? How looked he? Wherein went he?[18] What makes he here? Did he ask for me? Where remains he? How parted he with thee? and when shalt thou see him again? Answer me in one word.

Cel.   You must borrow me Gargantua's mouth[19] first: 't is a word too great for any mouth of this age's size. To say ay and no to these particulars is more than to answer in a catechism.

Ros.   But doth he know that I am in this forest and in man's apparel? Looks he as freshly as he did the day he wrestled?

Cel.   It is as easy to count atomies[20] as to resolve the propositions of a lover; but take a taste of my finding him, and relish it with good observance. I found him under a tree, like a dropped acorn.

Ros.   It may well be called Jove's tree,[21] when it drops forth such fruit.

Cel.   Give me audience, good madam.

Ros.   Proceed.

Cel.   There lay he, stretched along, like a wounded knight.

Ros.   Though it be pity to see such a sight, it well becomes the ground.

Cel.   Cry "holla"[22] to thy tongue, I prithee; it curvets unseasonably. He was furnished like a hunter.

Ros.   O, ominous! he comes to kill my heart.[23]

Cel.   I would sing my song without a burden: thou bringest me out of tune.

Ros.   Do you not know I am a woman? when I think, I must speak. Sweet, say on.

Cel.   You bring me out. Soft! comes he not here?

Enter ORLANDO *and* JAQUES

Ros.   'T is he: slink by, and note him.

---

[18]*Wherein went he?*] How did he go dressed?

[19]*Gargantua's mouth*] Gargantua, Rabelais' giant, swallows five pilgrims with their staves in a salad (Bk. I, ch. 38). Cf. Cotgrave's *Fr.-Engl. Dict.*, "Gargantua. Great throat, Rab."

[20]*atomies*] The Third and Fourth Folios read *atomes*, which Rowe changed to *atoms*. "Atomies" is used again in III, v, 13, *infra*.

[21]*Jove's tree*] Latin poets call the oak "Jove's tree." Shakespeare here seems to have borrowed direct from Golding's Ovid, *Met.*, I, 106: "The *acornes dropt* on ground from *Joves brode tree* in feelde."

[22]*"holla"*] stop! Cf. *Venus and Adonis*, 283–284: "What recketh he the rider's angry stir, His flattering 'Holla,' or his 'Stand, I say'?"

[23]*heart*] A common quibble between "heart" and "hart."

JAQ.   I thank you for your company; but, good faith, I had as lief have been myself alone.

ORL.   And so had I; but yet, for fashion sake, I thank you too for your society.

JAQ.   God buy you:[24] let's meet as little as we can.

ORL.   I do desire we may be better strangers.

JAQ.   I pray you, mar no more trees with writing love-songs in their barks.

ORL.   I pray you, mar no moe[25] of my verses with reading them ill-favouredly.

JAQ.   Rosalind is your love's name?

ORL.   Yes, just.

JAQ.   I do not like her name.

ORL.   There was no thought of pleasing you when she was christened.

JAQ.   What stature is she of?

ORL.   Just as high as my heart.

JAQ.   You are full of pretty answers. Have you not been acquainted with goldsmiths' wives, and conned them out of rings?[26]

ORL.   Not so; but I answer you right painted cloth,[27] from whence you have studied your questions.

JAQ.   You have a nimble wit: I think 't was made of Atalanta's heels.[28] Will you sit down with me? and we two will rail against our mistress the world, and all our misery.

ORL.   I will chide no breather[29] in the world but myself, against whom I know most faults.

JAQ.   The worst fault you have is to be in love.

ORL.   'T is a fault I will not change for your best virtue. I am weary of you.

JAQ.   By my troth, I was seeking for a fool when I found you.

ORL.   He is drowned in the brook: look but in, and you shall see him.

JAQ.   There I shall see mine own figure.

ORL.   Which I take to be either a fool or a cipher.

---

[24]*God buy you*] *buy* is the reading of the Folios. It is equivalent to "God b' wi' you," *i.e.*, "God be with you." Jaques repeats it, IV, i, 28, *infra*, and Touchstone in V, iv, 37.

[25]*moe*] This is the reading of the First Folio, which the later Folios change to the modern *more*.

[26]*goldsmiths' . . . rings*] Goldsmiths dealt largely at the time in rings on which were inscribed posies or mottoes.

[27]*right painted cloth*] Painted cloth was the term applied to cheap tapestries, on which tales from scripture or from popular literature were represented together with moral maxims or mottoes. Labels bearing brief speeches were sometimes attached to the mouths of the figures. Such speeches Orlando charges Jaques with studying. Cf., for a similar construction, line 199, *supra*, "*speak sad brow* and true maid."

[28]*Atalanta's heels*] Cf. note on line 137, *supra* (see footnote 10).

[29]*breather*] Cf. *Sonnet* lxxxi, 12: "When all the *breathers of this world* are dead."

JAQ. I'll tarry no longer with you: farewell, good Signior Love.

ORL. I am glad of your departure: adieu, good Monsieur Melancholy.

[*Exit* JAQUES.

ROS. [*Aside to* CELIA] I will speak to him like a saucy lackey, and under that habit play the knave with him. Do you hear, forester?

ORL. Very well: what would you?

ROS. I pray you, what is 't o'clock?

ORL. You should ask me what time o' day: there's no clock in the forest.

ROS. Then there is no true lover in the forest; else sighing every minute and groaning every hour would detect the lazy foot of Time as well as a clock.

ORL. And why not the swift foot of Time? had not that been as proper?

ROS. By no means, sir: Time travels in divers paces with divers persons. I'll tell you who Time ambles withal, who Time trots withal, who Time gallops withal and who he stands still withal.

ORL. I prithee, who doth he trot withal?

ROS. Marry, he trots hard with a young maid between the contract of her marriage and the day it is solemnized: if the interim be but a se'nnight, Time's pace is so hard that it seems the length of seven year.

ORL. Who ambles Time withal?

ROS. With a priest that lacks Latin, and a rich man that hath not the gout; for the one sleeps easily because he cannot study, and the other lives merrily because he feels no pain; the one lacking the burden of lean and wasteful learning, the other knowing no burden of heavy tedious penury: these Time ambles withal.

ORL. Who doth he gallop withal?

ROS. With a thief to the gallows; for though he go as softly as foot can fall, he thinks himself too soon there.

ORL. Who stays it still withal?

ROS. With lawyers in the vacation; for they sleep between term and term and then they perceive not how Time moves.

ORL. Where dwell you, pretty youth?

ROS. With this shepherdess, my sister: here in the skirts of the forest, like fringe upon a petticoat.

ORL. Are you native of this place?

ROS. As the cony that you see dwell where she is kindled.

ORL. Your accent is something finer than you could purchase in so removed a dwelling.

ROS. I have been told so of many: but indeed an old religious uncle of mine taught me to speak, who was in his youth an inland[30] man; one that knew courtship too well, for there he fell in love. I have heard him read many lectures against it, and I thank God I am not a woman, to be touched with so many giddy offences as he hath generally taxed their whole sex withal.

ORL. Can you remember any of the principal evils that he laid to the charge of women?

ROS. There were none principal; they were all like one another as half-pence are, every one fault seeming monstrous till his fellow-fault came to match it.

ORL. I prithee, recount some of them.

ROS. No, I will not cast away my physic but on those that are sick. There is a man haunts the forest, that abuses our young plants with carving Rosalind on their barks; hangs odes upon hawthorns and elegies on brambles; all, forsooth, deifying the name of Rosalind: if I could meet that fancy-monger, I would give him some good counsel, for he seems to have the quotidian of love[31] upon him.

ORL. I am he that is so love-shaked: I pray you, tell me your remedy.

ROS. There is none of my uncle's marks upon you: he taught me how to know a man in love; in which cage[32] of rushes I am sure you are not prisoner.

ORL. What were his marks?

ROS. A lean cheek, which you have not; a blue eye[33] and sunken, which you have not; an unquestionable[34] spirit, which you have not; a beard neglected, which you have not; but I pardon you for that, for simply your having in beard is a younger brother's revenue: then your hose should be ungartered, your bonnet unbanded,[35] your sleeve unbuttoned, your shoe untied and every thing about you demonstrating a careless desolation; but you are no such man; you are rather point-device in your accoutrements, as loving yourself than seeming the lover of any other.

[30]*inland*] refined. Cf. II, vii, 96, *supra*, "*inland* bred."

[31]*fancy-monger . . . quotidian of love*] Cf. Lyly's *Euphues* (p. 66): "If euer she haue been taken with the feuer of *fancie* [*i.e.*, love], she will help his ague, who by his *quotidian fit* [*i.e.*, daily recurring paroxysm of fever] is conuerted into phrensie."

[32]*cage*] often used for "prison." Rosalind mockingly suggests that Orlando's prison has rushes for bars, and is no serious impediment.

[33]*blue eye*] eye with a dark circle around it. Cf. *Tempest*, I, ii, 269: "*blue-eyed* hag."

[34]*unquestionable*] averse to conversation. Cf. *Hamlet*, I, iv, 43, "Thou comest in such a *questionable* shape," where "questionable" means "inciting to conversation," "willing to be conversed with."

[35]*bonnet unbanded*] Hats without hatbands were at the time regarded as signs of slovenliness in dress.

ORL.   Fair youth, I would I could make thee believe I love.

ROS.   Me believe it! you may as soon make her that you love believe
        it; which, I warrant, she is apter to do than to confess she does: that
        is one of the points in the which women still give the lie to their
        consciences. But, in good sooth, are you he that hangs the verses
        on the trees, wherein Rosalind is so admired?

ORL.   I swear to thee, youth, by the white hand of Rosalind, I am that
        he, that unfortunate he.

ROS.   But are you so much in love as your rhymes speak?

ORL.   Neither rhyme nor reason can express how much.

ROS.   Love is merely a madness; and, I tell you, deserves as well a dark
        house and a whip as madmen do:[36] and the reason why they are
        not so punished and cured is, that the lunacy is so ordinary that
        the whippers are in love too. Yet I profess curing it by counsel.

ORL.   Did you ever cure any so?

ROS.   Yes, one, and in this manner. He was to imagine me his love,
        his mistress; and I set him every day to woo me: at which time
        would I, being but a moonish youth, grieve, be effeminate,
        changeable, longing and liking; proud, fantastical, apish, shallow,
        inconstant, full of tears, full of smiles; for every passion something
        and for no passion truly any thing, as boys and women are for the
        most part cattle of this colour: would now like him, now loathe
        him; then entertain him, then forswear him; now weep for him,
        then spit at him; that I drave my suitor from his mad humour of
        love to a living[37] humour of madness; which was, to forswear the
        full stream of the world and to live in a nook merely monastic.
        And thus I cured him; and this way will I take upon me to wash
        your liver as clean as a sound sheep's heart, that there shall not be
        one spot of love in 't.

ORL.   I would not be cured, youth.

ROS.   I would cure you, if you would but call me Rosalind and come
        every day to my cote and woo me.

ORL.   Now, by the faith of my love, I will: tell me where it is.

ROS.   Go with me to it and I'll show it you: and by the way you shall
        tell me where in the forest you live. Will you go?

ORL.   With all my heart, good youth.

ROS.   Nay, you must call me Rosalind. Come, sister, will you go?
                                                              [*Exeunt.*

---

[36]*a dark house and a whip as madmen do*] this was the ordinary treatment of lunatics at
   the time. Cf. Malvolio's experience in *Tw. Night*, V, i.

[37]*mad . . . living*] unreasoning . . . real or actual.

SCENE III. *The Forest.*

Enter TOUCHSTONE *and* AUDREY; JAQUES *behind*

TOUCH. Come apace, good Audrey: I will fetch up your goats, Audrey. And how, Audrey? am I the man yet? doth my simple feature content you?

AUD. Your features![1] Lord warrant us! what features?

TOUCH. I am here with thee and thy goats, as the most capricious poet, honest Ovid, was among the Goths.[2]

JAQ. [*Aside*] O knowledge ill-inhabited, worse than Jove in a thatched house![3]

TOUCH. When a man's verses cannot be understood, nor a man's good wit seconded with the forward child, understanding, it strikes a man more dead than a great reckoning in a little room.[4] Truly, I would the gods had made thee poetical.

AUD. I do not know what "poetical" is: is it honest in deed and word? is it a true thing?

TOUCH. No, truly; for the truest poetry is the most feigning; and lovers are given to poetry, and what they swear in poetry may be said as lovers they do feign.

AUD. Do you wish then that the gods had made me poetical?

TOUCH. I do, truly; for thou swearest to me thou art honest: now, if thou wert a poet, I might have some hope thou didst feign.

AUD. Would you not have me honest?

TOUCH. No, truly, unless thou wert hard-favoured; for honesty coupled to beauty is to have honey a sauce to sugar.

JAQ. [*Aside*] A material fool!

AUD. Well, I am not fair; and therefore I pray the gods make me honest.

---

[1]*feature . . . features?*] This word was used in the three senses of (1) comeliness, (2) the build of the body, and (3) any part of the face. Touchstone apparently employs it in the first sense, and Audrey in the last. It is possible that there is an implied pun in Audrey's "what features?" on the word "faitor," *i.e.*, a villain, with which "feature" might easily be confused in pronunciation.

[2]*capricious . . . Goths*] "Capricious" is of course from the Latin "caper," a goat. "Goths" was so pronounced as to make the pun on "goats" quite clear. As a matter of history, Ovid was banished to the land of the Getae.

[3]*Jove . . . house*] The reference is to the thatched cottage of the peasants Philemon and Baucis, who entertained Jove unawares, according to Ovid, *Metam.*, VIII, 630, *seq.* There is another allusion to the story in *Much Ado*, II, i, 82–83: (D. Pedro.) "My visor is *Philemon's roof*; within the house is *Jove*. (Hero.) Why then, your visor should be *thatched*."

[4]*great reckoning . . . room*] a heavy bill for a narrow accommodation.

TOUCH. Truly, and to cast away honesty upon a foul slut were to put good meat into an unclean dish.

AUD. I am not a slut, though I thank the gods I am foul.[5]

TOUCH. Well, praised be the gods for thy foulness! sluttishness may come hereafter. But be it as it may be, I will marry thee, and to that end I have been with Sir Oliver Martext the vicar of the next village, who hath promised to meet me in this place of the forest and to couple us.

JAQ. [Aside] I would fain see this meeting.

AUD. Well, the gods give us joy!

TOUCH. Amen. A man may, if he were of a fearful heart, stagger in this attempt; for here we have no temple but the wood, no assembly but horn-beasts. But what though? Courage! As horns are odious, they are necessary. It is said, "many a man knows no end of his goods:" right; many a man has good horns, and knows no end of them. Well, that is the dowry of his wife; 't is none of his own getting. Horns?—even so:—poor men alone?[6] No, no; the noblest deer hath them as huge as the rascal. Is the single man therefore blessed? No: as a walled town is more worthier than a village, so is the forehead of a married man more honourable than the bare brow of a bachelor; and by how much defence[7] is better than no skill, by so much is a horn more precious than to want. Here comes Sir Oliver.

Enter SIR OLIVER MARTEXT

Sir Oliver Martext, you are well met: will you dispatch us here under this tree, or shall we go with you to your chapel?

SIR OLI. Is there none here to give the woman?

TOUCH. I will not take her on gift of any man.

SIR OLI. Truly, she must be given, or the marriage is not lawful.

JAQ. Proceed, proceed: I'll give her.

TOUCH. Good even, good Master What-ye-call 't: how do you, sir? You are very well met: God 'ild[8] you for your last company: I am very glad to see you: even a toy in hand here, sir: nay, pray be covered.

JAQ. Will you be married, motley?

---

[5]*foul*] the word meant "plain" or "homely," more frequently than "base" or "dirty." It was the ordinary antithesis of "fair."

[6]*Horns? . . . alone?*] The Folios read: *hornes, euen so poore men alone.* Theobald introduced the punctuation adopted in the text, which makes the passage intelligible.

[7]*defence*] art of fencing. Cf. *Hamlet*, IV, vii, 97: "art and exercise in your *defence*."

[8]*God 'ild*] God yield or reward you. The phrase is repeated by Touchstone, V, iv, 53, *infra*. Cf. *Ant. and Cleop.*, IV, ii, 33: "And the *gods yield* you for 't."

TOUCH.　As the ox hath his bow,[9] sir, the horse his curb and the falcon her bells, so man hath his desires; and as pigeons bill, so wed-
lock would be nibbling.

JAQ.　And will you, being a man of your breeding, be married under a
bush like a beggar? Get you to church, and have a good priest that
can tell you what marriage is: this fellow will but join you together
as they join wainscot; then one of you will prove a shrunk panel,
and like green timber warp, warp.

TOUCH. [*Aside*]　I am not in the mind but I were better to be married
of him than of another: for he is not like to marry me well; and not
being well married, it will be a good excuse for me hereafter to
leave my wife.

JAQ.　Go thou with me, and let me counsel thee.

TOUCH.　Come, sweet Audrey:
We must be married, or we must live in bawdry.
Farewell, good Master Oliver: not, —

O sweet Oliver,[10]
O brave Oliver,
Leave me not behind thee:

but, —

Wind away,[11]
Begone, I say,
I will not to wedding with thee.

[*Exeunt* JAQUES, TOUCHSTONE, *and* AUDREY.

SIR OLI.　'T is no matter: ne'er a fantastical knave of them all shall
flout me out of my calling.　　　　　　　　　　　　[*Exit.*

---

[9]*bow*] literally the bow-shaped piece of wood, which fitted into the yoke beneath the
neck of oxen, but here apparently used for the yoke itself.

[10]*O sweet Oliver*] This was the opening line of a very popular ballad. Only the two lines
("O swete Olyuer Leaue me not behind the[e]") survive elsewhere — in the license for
the publication of the ballad granted by the Stationers' Company to Richard Jones, 6
August, 1584.

[11]*Wind away*] Wend away, depart.

SCENE IV. *The Forest.*

Enter ROSALIND *and* CELIA

ROS.   Never talk to me; I will weep.

CEL.   Do, I prithee; but yet have the grace to consider that tears do not become a man.

ROS.   But have I not cause to weep?

CEL.   As good cause as one would desire; therefore weep.

ROS.   His very hair is of the dissembling colour.

CEL.   Something browner than Judas's:[1] marry, his kisses are Judas's own children.

ROS.   I' faith, his hair is of a good colour.

CEL.   An excellent colour: your chestnut was ever the only colour.

ROS.   And his kissing is as full of sanctity as the touch of holy bread.

CEL.   He hath bought a pair of cast[2] lips of Diana: a nun of winter's sisterhood kisses not more religiously; the very ice of chastity is in them.

ROS.   But why did he swear he would come this morning, and comes not?

CEL.   Nay, certainly, there is no truth in him.

ROS.   Do you think so?

CEL.   Yes; I think he is not a pick-purse nor a horse-stealer; but for his verity in love, I do think him as concave as a covered goblet[3] or a worm-eaten nut.

ROS.   Not true in love?

CEL.   Yes, when he is in; but I think he is not in.

ROS.   You have heard him swear downright he was.

CEL.   "Was" is not "is": besides, the oath of a lover is no stronger than the word of a tapster; they are both the confirmer of false reckonings. He attends here in the forest on the Duke your father.

ROS.   I met the Duke yesterday and had much question with him: he asked me of what parentage I was; I told him, of as good as he; so he laughed and let me go. But what talk we of fathers, when there is such a man as Orlando?

CEL.   O, that's a brave man! he writes brave verses, speaks brave

---

[1]*browner than Judas's*] Judas was invariably credited with red hair and beard.

[2]*cast*] This is the reading of the First Folio, but the other Folios read *chast*, i.e., chaste. "Cast" was frequently applied to apparel in the sense of "cast off," "left off." This epithet is more in keeping with Celia's banter than the conventional "chaste," which the mention of Diana naturally suggests.

[3]*concave . . . goblet*] a goblet when empty was kept covered.

words, swears brave oaths and breaks them bravely, quite traverse, athwart the heart of his lover; as a puisny[4] tilter, that spurs his horse but on one side, breaks his staff[5] like a noble goose: but all's brave that youth mounts and folly guides. Who comes here?

Enter CORIN

COR.   Mistress and master, you have oft inquired
After the shepherd that complain'd of love,
Who you saw sitting by me on the turf,
Praising the proud disdainful shepherdess
That was his mistress.
CEL.   Well, and what of him?
COR.   If you will see a pageant truly play'd,
Between the pale complexion of true love
And the red glow of scorn and proud disdain,
Go hence a little and I shall conduct you,
If you will mark it.
ROS.   O come, let us remove:
The sight of lovers feedeth those in love.
Bring us to this sight, and you shall say
I'll prove a busy actor in their play.
                                                                      [*Exeunt.*

SCENE V. *Another Part of the Forest.*

Enter SILVIUS *and* PHEBE

SIL.   Sweet Phebe, do not scorn me; do not, Phebe;
Say that you love me not, but say not so
In bitterness. The common executioner,
Whose heart the accustom'd sight of death makes hard,
Falls not the axe upon the humbled neck

---

[4]*puisny*] This is the old reading. Capell and later editors substitute the more modern form *puny*. It is used here not in the modern sense of "diminutive," but in that of "having the skill of a novice," "unskilled." The word comes through the French from the Latin "postnatus," "younger-born."

[5]*breaks his staff*] To break a staff in a tournament across ("quite traverse, athwart," l. 38) the body of an adversary, and not at push of point, was an accepted sign of clumsy incompetence. Cf. *All's Well*, II, i, 66, "Good faith, *across*," and *Much Ado*, V, i, 136–137: "this last [staff] was broke *cross*."

But first begs pardon: will you sterner be
Than he that dies and lives[1] by bloody drops?

Enter ROSALIND, CELIA, *and* CORIN, *behind*

PHE.   I would not be thy executioner:
I fly thee, for I would not injure thee.
Thou tell'st me there is murder in mine eye:
'T is pretty, sure, and very probable,
That eyes, that are the frail'st and softest things,
Who shut their coward gates on atomies,[2]
Should be call'd tyrants, butchers, murderers!
Now I do frown on thee with all my heart;
And if mine eyes can wound, now let them kill thee:
Now counterfeit to swoon; why now fall down;
Or if thou canst not, O, for shame, for shame,
Lie not, to say mine eyes are murderers!
Now show the wound mine eye hath made in thee:
Scratch thee but with a pin, and there remains
Some scar of it; lean but upon a rush,
The cicatrice and capable impressure[3]
Thy palm some moment keeps; but now mine eyes,
Which I have darted at thee, hurt thee not,
Nor, I am sure, there is no force in eyes
That can do hurt.
SIL.   O dear Phebe,
If ever,—as that ever may be near,—
You meet in some fresh cheek the power of fancy,
Then shall you know the wounds invisible
That love's keen arrows make.
PHE.   But till that time
Come not thou near me: and when that time comes,
Afflict me with thy mocks, pity me not;
As till that time I shall not pity thee.
ROS.   And why, I pray you? Who might be your mother,
That you insult, exult, and all at once,
Over the wretched? What though you have no beauty,—
As, by my faith, I see no more in you
Than without candle may go dark to bed,—

---

[1]*dies and lives*] This is a common inversion of the more ordinary phrase "lives and dies,"
i.e., subsists from the cradle to the grave. Cf. Barclay's *Ship of Fooles*, 1570, f. 67: "He
is a foole, and so shall he *dye and live*."
[2]*atomies*] Cf. III, ii, 217, *supra*.
[3]*The cicatrice . . . impressure*] The scar, or mark, and perceptible or sensible impression.

Must you be therefore proud and pitiless?
Why, what means this? Why do you look on me?
I see no more in you than in the ordinary
Of nature's sale-work.[4] 'Od's my little life,
I think she means to tangle my eyes too!
No, faith, proud mistress, hope not after it:
'T is not your inky brows, your black silk hair,
Your bugle[5] eyeballs, nor your cheek of cream,
That can entame my spirits to your worship.
You foolish shepherd, wherefore do you follow her,
Like foggy south, puffing with wind and rain?[6]
You are a thousand times a properer man
Than she a woman: 't is such fools as you
That makes the world full of ill-favour'd children:
'T is not her glass, but you, that flatters her;
And out of you she sees herself more proper
Than any of her lineaments can show her.
But, mistress, know yourself: down on your knees,
And thank heaven, fasting, for a good man's love:
For I must tell you friendly in your ear,
Sell when you can: you are not for all markets:
Cry the man mercy; love him; take his offer:
Foul is most foul, being foul to be a scoffer.[7]
So take her to thee, shepherd: fare you well.

PHE.　Sweet youth, I pray you, chide a year together:
I had rather hear you chide than this man woo.

Ros.　He's fallen in love with your foulness and she'll fall in love with
my anger. If it be so, as fast as she answers thee with frowning
looks, I'll sauce her with bitter words. Why look you so upon me?

PHE.　For no ill will I bear you.

Ros.　I pray you, do not fall in love with me,
For I am falser than vows made in wine:
Besides, I like you not. If you will know my house,
'T is at the tuft of olives here hard by.
Will you go, sister? Shepherd, ply her hard.
Come, sister. Shepherdess, look on him better,
And be not proud: though all the world could see,

---

[4]*sale-work*] ready-made goods.
[5]*bugle*] black, from the tube-shaped glass bead, commonly of that colour, used to or-
nament wearing apparel.
[6]*foggy south . . . rain*] The foggy southern quarter of the sky, which generates wind and
rain. Cf. *Rom. and Jul.,* I, iv, 103: "the *dewdropping south.*"
[7]*Foul . . . scoffer*] An ugly woman exaggerates her ugliness when she grows scornful.

None could be so abused in sight as he.
Come, to our flock.   [*Exeunt* ROSALIND, CELIA, *and* CORIN.
PHE.   Dead shepherd, now I find thy saw of might,
    "Who ever loved that loved not at first sight?"[8]
SIL.   Sweet Phebe,—
PHE.   Ha, what say'st thou, Silvius?
SIL.   Sweet Phebe, pity me.
PHE.   Why, I am sorry for thee, gentle Silvius.
SIL.   Wherever sorrow is, relief would be:
    If you do sorrow at my grief in love,
    By giving love your sorrow and my grief
    Were both extermined.
PHE.   Thou hast my love: is not that neighbourly?
SIL.   I would have you.
PHE.   Why, that were covetousness.
    Silvius, the time was that I hated thee,
    And yet it is not that I bear thee love;
    But since that thou canst talk of love so well,
    Thy company, which erst was irksome to me,
    I will endure, and I'll employ thee too:
    But do not look for further recompense
    Than thine own gladness that thou art employ'd.
SIL.   So holy and so perfect is my love,
    And I in such a poverty of grace,
    That I shall think it a most plenteous crop
    To glean the broken ears after the man
    That the main harvest reaps: loose now and then
    A scatter'd smile, and that I'll live upon.
PHE.   Know'st thou the youth that spoke to me erewhile?
SIL.   Not very well, but I have met him oft;
    And he hath bought the cottage and the bounds
    That the old carlot[9] once was master of.
PHE.   Think not I love him, though I ask for him;
    'T is but a peevish boy; yet he talks well;
    But what care I for words? yet words do well
    When he that speaks them pleases those that hear.
    It is a pretty youth: not very pretty:

[8]*Dead shepherd . . . sight*] The "dead shepherd" is Christopher Marlowe, who died in 1593. The line, "Who ever loved," etc., is from Marlowe's popular translation of the pseudo-Musaeus' Greek poem, *Hero and Leander* (Sest. I, l. 176), first printed in 1598.

[9]*carlot*] Apparently a diminutive of "carl," churl, peasant. No other example of the word is found.

But, sure, he's proud, and yet his pride becomes him:
He'll make a proper man: the best thing in him
Is his complexion; and faster than his tongue
Did make offence his eye did heal it up.
He is not very tall; yet for his years he's tall:
His leg is but so so; and yet 't is well:
There was a pretty redness in his lip,
A little riper and more lusty red
Than that mix'd in his cheek; 't was just the difference
Betwixt the constant red and mingled damask.[10]
There be some women, Silvius, had they mark'd him
In parcels as I did, would have gone near
To fall in love with him: but, for my part,
I love him not nor hate him not; and yet
I have more cause to hate him than to love him:
For what had he to do to chide at me?
He said mine eyes were black and my hair black;
And, now I am remember'd, scorn'd at me:
I marvel why I answer'd not again:
But that's all one; omittance is no quittance.[11]
I'll write to him a very taunting letter,
And thou shalt bear it: wilt thou, Silvius?

SIL.　　Phebe, with all my heart.

PHE.　　　　　　　　　　I'll write it straight;
The matter 's in my head and in my heart:
I will be bitter with him and passing short.
Go with me, Sylvius.　　　　　　　　　　[*Exeunt.*

---

[10]*mingled damask*] Cf. *Sonnet* cxxx, 5: "I have seen roses *damask'd*, red and white."
[11]*omittance is no quittance*] Milton, *Paradise Lost*, X, 53, varies this expression thus: "Forbearance is no quittance." Quittance means discharge.

ACT IV.

SCENE I. *The Forest.*

Enter ROSALIND, CELIA, *and* JAQUES

JAQUES. I prithee, pretty youth, let me be better acquainted with thee.

ROS. They say you are a melancholy fellow.

JAQ. I am so; I do love it better than laughing.

ROS. Those that are in extremity of either are abominable fellows, and betray themselves to every modern censure[1] worse than drunkards.

JAQ. Why, 't is good to be sad and say nothing.

ROS. Why then, 't is good to be a post.

JAQ. I have neither the scholar's melancholy, which is emulation; nor the musician's, which is fantastical; nor the courtier's, which is proud; nor the soldier's, which is ambitious; nor the lawyer's, which is politic; nor the lady's, which is nice; nor the lover's, which is all these: but it is a melancholy of mine own, compounded of many simples, extracted from many objects; and indeed the sundry contemplation of my travels, in which my often rumination wraps me in a most humorous sadness.

ROS. A traveller! By my faith, you have great reason to be sad: I fear you have sold your own lands to see other men's; then, to have seen much, and to have nothing, is to have rich eyes[2] and poor hands.

JAQ. Yes, I have gained my experience.

ROS. And your experience makes you sad: I had rather have a fool to make me merry than experience to make me sad; and to travel for it too!

Enter ORLANDO

[1]*modern censure*] common, ordinary judgment.
[2]*rich eyes*] Cf. *All's Well*, V, iii, 16–17: "the survey Of *richest eyes*."

ORL.   Good day and happiness, dear Rosalind!

JAQ.   Nay, then, God buy you,[3] an you talk in blank verse.   [*Exit.*

ROS.   Farewell, Monsieur Traveller: look you lisp and wear strange
suits; disable all the benefits of your own country; be out of love
with your nativity and almost chide God for making you that
countenance you are; or I will scarce think you have swam in a
gondola[4] Why, how now, Orlando! where have you been all this
while? You a lover! An you serve me such another trick, never
come in my sight more.

ORL.   My fair Rosalind, I come within an hour of my promise.

ROS.   Break an hour's promise in love! He that will divide a minute
into a thousand parts, and break but a part of the thousandth part
of a minute in the affairs of love, it may be said of him that Cupid
hath clapped him o' the shoulder, but I'll warrant him heart-
whole.

ORL.   Pardon me, dear Rosalind.

ROS.   Nay, an you be so tardy, come no more in my sight: I had as lief
be wooed of a snail.

ORL.   Of a snail?

ROS.   Ay, of a snail; for though he comes slowly, he carries his house
on his head; a better jointure, I think, than you make a woman:
besides, he brings his destiny with him.

ORL.   What's that?

ROS.   Why, horns, which such as you are fain to be beholding to your
wives for: but he comes armed in his fortune and prevents the
slander of his wife.

ORL.   Virtue is no horn-maker; and my Rosalind is virtuous.

ROS.   And I am your Rosalind.

CEL.   It pleases him to call you so; but he hath a Rosalind of a better
leer than you.

ROS.   Come, woo me, woo me; for now I am in a holiday humour and
like enough to consent. What would you say to me now, an I were
your very very Rosalind?

ORL.   I would kiss before I spoke.

ROS.   Nay, you were better speak first; and when you were gravelled
for lack of matter, you might take occasion to kiss. Very good ora-
tors, when they are out, they will spit; and for lovers lacking—God
warn us!—matter, the cleanliest shift is to kiss.

ORL.   How if the kiss be denied?

ROS.   Then she puts you to entreaty and there begins new matter.

---

[3]*God buy you*] Cf. III, ii, 242, *supra.*

[4]*swam in a gondola*] been on a visit to Venice, the fashionable goal of contemporary
travel.

ORL.   Who could be out, being before his beloved mistress?

ROS.   Marry, that should you, if I were your mistress, or I should think my honesty ranker than my wit.

ORL.   What, of my suit?

ROS.   Not out of your apparel, and yet out of your suit. Am not I your Rosalind?

ORL.   I take some joy to say you are, because I would be talking of her.

ROS.   Well, in her person, I say I will not have you.

ORL.   Then in mine own person I die.

ROS.   No, faith, die by attorney.[5] The poor world is almost six thousand years old, and in all this time there was not any man died in his own person, videlicet, in a love-cause. Troilus had his brains dashed out with a Grecian club; yet he did what he could to die before, and he is one of the patterns of love. Leander, he would have lived many a fair year, though Hero had turned nun, if it had not been for a hot midsummer night; for, good youth, he went but forth to wash him in the Hellespont and being taken with the cramp was drowned: and the foolish chroniclers[6] of that age found it was "Hero of Sestos." But these are all lies: men have died from time to time and worms have eaten them, but not for love.

ORL.   I would not have my right Rosalind of this mind; for, I protest, her frown might kill me.

ROS.   By this hand, it will not kill a fly. But come, now I will be your Rosalind in a more coming-on disposition, and ask me what you will, I will grant it.

ORL.   Then love me, Rosalind.

ROS.   Yes, faith, will I, Fridays and Saturdays and all.

ORL.   And wilt thou have me?

ROS.   Ay, and twenty such.

ORL.   What sayest thou?

ROS.   Are you not good?

ORL.   I hope so.

ROS.   Why then, can one desire too much of a good thing? Come, sister, you shall be the priest and marry us. Give me your hand, Orlando. What do you say, sister?

ORL.   Pray thee, marry us.

CEL.   I cannot say the words.

ROS.   You must begin, "Will you, Orlando—"

[5]*by attorney*] by deputy. Cf. *Rich. III*, V, iii, 83: "I, *by attorney*, bless thee from thy mother."

[6]*chroniclers*] This is the reading of the Folios. It was needlessly changed by Hanmer to *coroners*, which the use of the word "found," *i.e.* "gave the finding or verdict," only speciously supports.

CEL. Go to. Will you, Orlando, have to wife this Rosalind?

ORL. I will.

ROS. Ay, but when?

ORL. Why now; as fast as she can marry us.

ROS. Then you must say "I take thee, Rosalind, for wife."

ORL. I take thee, Rosalind, for wife.

ROS. I might ask you for your commission; but I do take thee, Orlando, for my husband: there's a girl goes before the priest;[7] and certainly a woman's thought runs before her actions.

ORL. So do all thoughts; they are winged.

ROS. Now tell me how long you would have her after you have possessed her.

ORL. For ever and a day.

ROS. Say "a day," without the "ever." No, no, Orlando, men are April when they woo, December when they wed: maids are May when they are maids, but the sky changes when they are wives. I will be more jealous of thee than a Barbary cock-pigeon[8] over his hen, more clamorous than a parrot against rain, more new-fangled[9] than an ape, more giddy in my desires than a monkey: I will weep for nothing, like Diana in the fountain,[10] and I will do that when you are disposed to be merry; I will laugh like a hyen, and that when thou art inclined to sleep.

ORL. But will my Rosalind do so?

ROS. By my life, she will do as I do.

ORL. O, but she is wise.

ROS. Or else she could not have the wit to do this: the wiser, the waywarder: make the doors upon a woman's wit and it will out at the casement; shut that and 't will out at the key-hole; stop that, 't will fly with the smoke out at the chimney.

ORL. A man that had a wife with such a wit, he might say "Wit, whither wilt?"[11]

ROS. Nay, you might keep that check for it till you met your wife's wit going to your neighbour's bed.

ORL. And what wit could wit have to excuse that?

---

[7]*there 's a girl . . . priest*] Rosalind admits that the bride is anticipating the part in the ceremony that belongs to Celia, who acts as priest.

[8]*Barbary cock-pigeon*] This bird, now known as a "barb," is of black colour, and was introduced from North Africa. Cf. *2 Hen. IV*, II, iv, 94: "*Barbary* hen."

[9]*new-fangled*] fond of what is new. Cf. Cotgrave's *Fr.-Eng. Dict.*: "Fantastique, humorous, *new-fangled*, giddie, skittish."

[10]*like . . . fountain*] A possible allusion to an "alabaster image of Diana," which, according to Stow, was set up near the cross at West Cheap, London, with "water conveyed from the Thames prilling from her naked breast."

[11]*Wit, whither wilt?*] Cf. I, ii, 51, *supra*.

Ros. Marry, to say she came to seek you there. You shall never take her without her answer, unless you take her without her tongue. O, that woman that cannot make her fault her husband's occasion,[12] let her never nurse her child herself, for she will breed it like a fool!

Orl. For these two hours, Rosalind, I will leave thee.

Ros. Alas, dear love, I cannot lack thee two hours!

Orl. I must attend the Duke at dinner: by two o'clock I will be with thee again.

Ros. Ay, go your ways, go your ways; I knew what you would prove: my friends told me as much, and I thought no less: that flattering tongue of yours won me: 't is but one cast away, and so, come, death! Two o'clock is your hour?

Orl. Ay, sweet Rosalind.

Ros. By my troth, and in good earnest, and so God mend me, and by all pretty oaths that are not dangerous, if you break one jot of your promise or come one minute behind your hour, I will think you the most pathetical[13] break-promise, and the most hollow lover, and the most unworthy of her you call Rosalind, that may be chosen out of the gross band of the unfaithful: therefore beware my censure and keep your promise.

Orl. With no less religion than if thou wert indeed my Rosalind: so adieu.

Ros. Well, Time is the old justice that examines all such offenders, and let Time try: adieu.   [Exit ORLANDO.

Cel. You have simply misused our sex in your love-prate: we must have your doublet and hose plucked over your head, and show the world what the bird hath done to her own nest.

Ros. O coz, coz, coz, my pretty little coz, that thou didst know how many fathom deep I am in love! But it cannot be sounded: my affection hath an unknown bottom, like the bay of Portugal.[14]

Cel. Or rather, bottomless; that as fast as you pour affection in, it runs out.

Ros. No, that same wicked bastard of Venus that was begot of thought, conceived of spleen, and born of madness, that blind

[12]*make . . . occasion*] represent her fault to be occasioned by her husband, or make her fault the opportunity of taking advantage of her husband. The reading, though often questioned, is probably right.

[13]*pathetical*] The word, though often meaning "impassioned," or "persuasive," seems to acquire here a touch of scorn, and is almost equivalent to "pitiful." Cf. *L. L. L.*, IV, i, 141: "A most *pathetical* wit."

[14]*bay of Portugal*] Sailors bestowed this title on the sea off the Portuguese coast between Oporto and Cintra. The water there attained a depth of 1400 fathoms within 42 miles of the shore.

rascally boy that abuses every one's eyes because his own are out,
let him be judge how deep I am in love. I'll tell thee, Aliena, I cannot be out of the sight of Orlando: I'll go find a shadow[15] and sigh
till he come.

CEL.　And I'll sleep.　　　　　　　　　　　　　　　　　　[*Exeunt.*

SCENE II. *The Forest.*

Enter JAQUES, Lords, *and* Foresters

JAQ.　Which is he that killed the deer?

A LORD.　Sir, it was I.

JAQ.　Let 's present him to the Duke, like a Roman conqueror; and it
　　would do well to set the deer's horns upon his head, for a branch
　　of victory. Have you no song, forester, for this purpose?

FOR.　Yes, sir.

JAQ.　Sing it: 't is no matter how it be in tune, so it make noise enough.

SONG

FOR.　　　　　　What shall he have that kill'd the deer?
　　　　　　　　His leather skin and horns to wear.
　　　　　　　　　Then sing him home:[1]
　　　　　　　　　　　　[*The rest shall bear this burden.*
　　　　　　　　Take thou no scorn to wear the horn;
　　　　　　　　It was a crest ere thou wast born:
　　　　　　　　　Thy father's father wore it,
　　　　　　　　　And thy father bore it:
　　　　　　　　The horn, the horn, the lusty horn
　　　　　　　　Is not a thing to laugh to scorn.　　　　[*Exeunt.*

---

[15]*shadow*] shade, or shady place. Cf. *Tempest*, IV, i, 66–67: "Broom-groves, Whose
　shadow the dismissed bachelor loves."

[1]*Then sing him home:*] In the Folios these words, together with those here printed as the
appended stage direction, form a single line of the song. Theobald first made the
change which is adopted here. A few editors read, *They sing him home,* and include
these words along with those which follow in the stage direction. The song appears
with music in John Hilton's *Catch that catch can,* 1652. The particular words with
which this note deals are all omitted. Hilton is doubtfully identified with a famous musician of the same name, who was Shakespeare's contemporary.

SCENE III. *The Forest.*

Enter ROSALIND *and* CELIA

ROS.   How say you now? Is it not past two o'clock? and here much
       Orlando![1]
CEL.   I warrant you, with pure love and troubled brain, he hath ta'en his
       bow and arrows and is gone forth to sleep. Look, who comes here.

Enter SILVIUS

SIL.   My errand is to you, fair youth;
       My gentle Phebe bid me give you this:
       I know not the contents: but, as I guess
       By the stern brow and waspish action
       Which she did use as she was writing of it,
       It bears an angry tenour: pardon me;
       I am but as a guiltless messenger.
ROS.   Patience herself would startle at this letter
       And play the swaggerer; bear this, bear all:
       She says I am not fair, that I lack manners;
       She calls me proud, and that she could not love me,
       Were man as rare as phœnix.[2] 'Od's my will!
       Her love is not the hare that I do hunt:
       Why writes she so to me? Well, shepherd, well,
       This is a letter of your own device.
SIL.   No, I protest, I know not the contents:
       Phebe did write it.
ROS.   Come, come, you are a fool,
       And turn'd into the extremity of love.
       I saw her hand: she has a leathern hand,
       A freestone-colour'd[3] hand; I verily did think
       That her old gloves were on, but 't was her hands:
       She has a huswife's hand; but that's no matter:
       I say she never did invent this letter;
       This is a man's invention and his hand.

[1] *and here much Orlando*] An ironical use of "much," implying just the opposite of what
the word means: "we find much of, a great deal of, Orlando here," *i.e.*, "he is not here
at all." Cf. the colloquialism, "I shall get much [*verè* — nothing] by that."
[2] *as rare as phœnix*] The phœnix is commonly described in classical poetry as unique.
Cf. Ovid's *Amores*, II, vi, 54, "vivax phœnix, *unica* semper avis." Cf. *Tempest*, III, iii,
23: "There is one tree, the phœnix' throne; *one phœnix*."
[3] *freestone-colour'd*] brownish yellow, like bath brick.

SIL.   Sure, it is hers.

ROS.   Why, 't is a boisterous and a cruel style,
      A style for challengers; why, she defies me,
      Like Turk to Christian: women's gentle brain
      Could not drop forth such giant-rude invention,
      Such Ethiope[4] words, blacker in their effect
      Than in their countenance. Will you hear the letter?

SIL.   So please you, for I never heard it yet;
      Yet heard too much of Phebe's cruelty.

ROS.   She Phebes me: mark how the tyrant writes.

[*Reads*]   Art thou god to shepherd turn'd,
                    That a maiden's heart hath burn'd?

Can a woman rail thus?

SIL.   Call you this railing?

ROS.   [*reads*]

                  Why, thy godhead laid apart,
                  Warr'st thou with a woman's heart?

Did you ever hear such railing?

                  Whiles the eye of man did woo me,
                  That could do no vengeance to me.

Meaning me a beast.

                  If the scorn of your bright eyne
                  Have power to raise such love in mine,
                  Alack, in me what strange effect
                  Would they work in mild aspect![5]
                  Whiles you chid me, I did love;
                  How then might your prayers move!
                  He that brings this love to thee
                  Little knows this love in me:
                  And by him seal up thy mind;[6]
                  Whether that thy youth and kind[7]
                  Will the faithful offer take
                  Of me and all that I can make;
                  Or else by him my love deny,
                  And then I'll study how to die.

---

[4] *Ethiope*] this is the only example of the adjectival use of this word, which is frequently found elsewhere as a noun, meaning "a swarthy person."

[5] *aspect*] This word, which is always accented on the last syllable in Shakespeare, is here an astrological term denoting the appearance of the planets. Cf. *Wint. Tale*, II, i, 106–107: "the heavens look With an *aspéct* more favourable."

[6] *seal up thy mind*] seal up your decision, and send it back by him.

[7] *youth and kind*] youth and nature, the natural sentiment of youth.

SIL.   Call you this chiding?

CEL.   Alas, poor shepherd!

ROS.   Do you pity him? no, he deserves no pity. Wilt thou love such
a woman? What, to make thee an instrument and play false strains
upon thee! not to be endured! Well, go your way to her, for I see
love hath made thee a tame snake, and say this to her: that if she
love me, I charge her to love thee; if she will not, I will never have
her unless thou entreat for her. If you be a true lover, hence, and
not a word; for here comes more company.   [*Exit* SILVIUS.

Enter OLIVER

OLI.   Good morrow, fair ones: pray you, if you know,
Where in the purlieus of this forest stands
A sheep-cote fenced about with olive-trees?

CEL.   West of this place, down in the neighbour bottom:
The rank of osiers by the murmuring stream
Left on your right hand brings you to the place.
But at this hour the house doth keep itself;
There 's none within.

OLI.   If that an eye may profit by a tongue,
Then should I know you by description;
Such garments and such years: "The boy is fair,
Of female favour, and bestows himself[8]
Like a ripe sister:[9] the woman low,
And browner than her brother." Are not you
The owner of the house I did inquire for?

CEL.   It is no boast, being ask'd, to say we are.

OLI.   Orlando doth commend him to you both,
And to that youth he calls his Rosalind
He sends this bloody napkin.[10] Are you he?

ROS.   I am: what must we understand by this?

OLI.   Some of my shame; if you will know of me
What man I am, and how, and why, and where
This handkercher was stain'd.

CEL.   I pray you, tell it.

OLI.   When last the young Orlando parted from you

---

[8]*bestows himself*] deports himself, behaves, as in *2 Hen. IV*, II, ii, 163–164: "How might
we see Falstaff *bestow himself* to-night in his true colours."

[9]*Like a ripe sister*] This, the original reading, leaves the line metrically imperfect. A syllable seems lacking after "sister." But such an irregularity is not uncommon. With a
view to correcting the metre, and removing the ambiguity of "ripe sister," *right forester*"
has been substituted. "Like a ripe sister" may be correct, and may mean that Rosalind
treats Celia like a mature, elder kinswoman.

[10]*napkin*] This is the "handkercher" or "handkerchief" of line 96, *infra*.

He left a promise to return again
Within an hour, and pacing through the forest,
Chewing the food of sweet and bitter fancy,
Lo, what befel! he threw his eye aside,
And mark what object did present itself:
Under an oak,[11] whose boughs were moss'd with age
And high top bald with dry antiquity,
A wretched ragged man, o'ergrown with hair,
Lay sleeping on his back: about his neck
A green and gilded snake had wreathed itself,
Who with her head nimble in threats approach'd
The opening of his mouth; but suddenly,
Seeing Orlando, it unlink'd itself,
And with indented glides[12] did slip away
Into a bush: under which bush's shade
A lioness, with udders all drawn dry,
Lay couching, head on ground, with catlike watch,
When that the sleeping man should stir; for 't is
The royal disposition of that beast
To prey on nothing that doth seem as dead:
This seen, Orlando did approach the man
And found it was his brother, his elder brother.

CEL.   O, I have heard him speak of that same brother;
And he did render him the most unnatural
That lived amongst men.

OLI.   And well he might so do,
For well I know he was unnatural.

ROS.   But, to Orlando: did he leave him there,
Food to the suck'd and hungry lioness?

OLI.   Twice did he turn his back and purposed so;
But kindness, nobler ever than revenge,
And nature, stronger than his just occasion,[13]
Made him give battle to the lioness,
Who quickly fell before him: in which hurtling
From miserable slumber I awaked.

CEL.   Are you his brother?

ROS.   Was 't you he rescued?

---

[11]*oak*] The Folios insert *old* before *oak*, but metrical considerations almost compel its omission, which Pope first proposed.

[12]*indented glides*] sinuous glidings. Cf. "*indented* wave" of the movement of the serpent in Milton's *Paradise Lost*, IX, 496.

[13]*just occasion*] the just ground which would have warranted Orlando in abandoning his brother.

CEL.   Was 't you that did so oft contrive to kill him?
OLI.   'T was I; but 't is not I: I do not shame
       To tell you what I was, since my conversion
       So sweetly tastes, being the thing I am.
ROS.   But, for the bloody napkin?
OLI.   By and by.
       When from the first to last betwixt us two
       Tears our recountments had most kindly bathed,
       As[14] how I came into that desert place;
       In brief, he led me to the gentle Duke,
       Who gave me fresh array and entertainment,
       Committing me unto my brother's love;
       Who led me instantly unto his cave,
       There stripp'd himself, and here upon his arm
       The lioness had torn some flesh away,
       Which all this while had bled; and now he fainted
       And cried, in fainting, upon Rosalind.
       Brief, I recover'd him, bound up his wound;
       And, after some small space, being strong at heart,
       He sent me hither, stranger as I am,
       To tell this story, that you might excuse
       His broken promise, and to give this napkin,
       Dyed in his blood, unto the shepherd youth
       That he in sport doth call his Rosalind.
                                   [ROSALIND *swoons.*
CEL.   Why, how now, Ganymede! sweet Ganymede!
OLI.   Many will swoon when they do look on blood.
CEL.   There is more in it. Cousin Ganymede!
OLI.   Look, he recovers.
ROS.   I would I were at home.
CEL.   We'll lead you thither.
       I pray you, will you take him by the arm?
OLI.   Be of good cheer, youth: you a man! you lack a man's heart.
ROS.   I do so, I confess it. Ah, sirrah, a body would think this was well
       counterfeited! I pray you, tell your brother how well I counter-
       feited. Heigh-ho!
OLI.   This was not counterfeit: there is too great testimony in your
       complexion that it was a passion of earnest.
ROS.   Counterfeit, I assure you.
OLI.   Well then, take a good heart and counterfeit to be a man.
ROS.   So I do: but, i' faith, I should have been a woman by right.

---

[14]As] As for instance.

CEL.　Come, you look paler and paler: pray you, draw homewards. Good sir, go with us.

OLI.　That will I, for I must bear answer back How you excuse my brother, Rosalind.

ROS.　I shall devise something: but, I pray you, commend my counterfeiting to him. Will you go?　　　　　　　　　　　　　[*Exeunt.*

ACT V.

SCENE I. *The Forest.*

Enter TOUCHSTONE *and* AUDREY

TOUCHSTONE.   We shall find a time, Audrey; patience, gentle Audrey.

AUD.   Faith, the priest was good enough, for all the old gentleman's saying.

TOUCH.   A most wicked Sir Oliver, Audrey, a most vile Martext. But, Audrey, there is a youth here in the forest lays claim to you.

AUD.   Ay, I know who 't is: he hath no interest in me in the world: here comes the man you mean.

TOUCH.   It is meat and drink[1] to me to see a clown: by my troth, we that have good wits have much to answer for; we shall be flouting; we cannot hold.[2]

Enter WILLIAM

WILL.   Good even, Audrey.

AUD.   God ye good even, William.

WILL.   And good even to you, sir.

TOUCH.   Good even, gentle friend. Cover thy head, cover thy head; nay, prithee, be covered. How old are you, friend?

WILL.   Five and twenty, sir.

TOUCH.   A ripe age. Is thy name William?

WILL.   William, sir.

TOUCH.   A fair name. Wast born i' the forest here?

WILL.   Ay, sir, I thank God.

TOUCH.   "Thank God;" a good answer. Art rich?

WILL.   Faith, sir, so so.

---

[1] *meat and drink*] a proverbial expression implying something very congenial. Cf. *M. Wives*, I, i, 268: "That's *meat and drink* to me."

[2] *hold*] restrain (*sc.* our wit).

TOUCH.   "So so" is good, very good, very excellent good; and yet it is
    not; it is but so so. Art thou wise?

WILL.   Ay, sir, I have a pretty wit.

TOUCH.   Why, thou sayest well. I do now remember a saying, "The
    fool doth think he is wise, but the wise man knows himself to be
    a fool." The heathen philosopher, when he had a desire to eat a
    grape, would open his lips when he put it into his mouth; mean-
    ing thereby that grapes were made to eat and lips to open. You do
    love this maid?

WILL.   I do, sir.

TOUCH.   Give me your hand. Art thou learned?

WILL.   No, sir.

TOUCH.   Then learn this of me: to have, is to have; for it is a fig-
    ure in rhetoric that drink, being poured out of a cup into a
    glass, by filling the one doth empty the other; for all your writ-
    ers do consent that ipse is he: now, you are not ipse, for I am
    he.

WILL.   Which he, sir?

TOUCH.   He, sir, that must marry this woman. Therefore, you
    clown, abandon,—which is in the vulgar leave,—the soci-
    ety,—which in the boorish is company,—of this female,—
    which in the common is woman; which together is, abandon
    the society of this female, or, clown, thou perishest; or, to thy
    better understanding, diest; or, to wit, I kill thee, make thee
    away, translate thy life into death, thy liberty into bondage: I
    will deal in poison with thee, or in bastinado,[3] or in steel; I
    will bandy[4] with thee in faction; I will o'er-run thee with pol-
    icy; I will kill thee a hundred and fifty ways: therefore tremble,
    and depart.

AUD.   Do, good William.

WILL.   God rest you merry, sir.   [*Exit.*

Enter CORIN

COR.   Our master and mistress seeks you; come, away, away!

TOUCH.   Trip, Audrey! trip, Audrey! I attend, I attend.   [*Exeunt.*

---

[3]*bastinado*] cudgelling. Cf. Florio's *Ital.-Eng. Dict.*: "A *bastonado*, or cudgell-blow."
[4]*bandy*] The word literally means "to toss from side to side like a tennis-ball"; but it is
    here synonymous with "contend" or "fight."

SCENE II. *The Forest.*

Enter ORLANDO *and* OLIVER

ORL.   Is 't possible that on so little acquaintance you should like her? that but seeing you should love her? and loving woo? and, wooing, she should grant? and will you persever to enjoy her?

OLI.   Neither call the giddiness of it in question, the poverty of her, the small acquaintance, my sudden wooing, nor her sudden consenting; but say with me, I love Aliena; say with her that she loves me; consent with both that we may enjoy each other: it shall be to your good; for my father's house and all the revenue that was old Sir Rowland's will I estate upon you, and here live and die a shepherd.

ORL.   You have my consent. Let your wedding be to-morrow: thither will I invite the Duke and all's contented followers. Go you and prepare Aliena; for look you, here comes my Rosalind.

Enter ROSALIND

ROS.   God save you, brother.

OLI.   And you, fair sister.[1]   [*Exit.*

ROS.   O, my dear Orlando, how it grieves me to see thee wear thy heart in a scarf![2]

ORL.   It is my arm.

ROS.   I thought thy heart had been wounded with the claws of a lion.

ORL.   Wounded it is, but with the eyes of a lady.

ROS.   Did your brother tell you how I counterfeited to swoon when he showed me your handkercher?

ORL.   Ay, and greater wonders than that.

ROS.   O, I know where you are: nay, 't is true: there was never any thing so sudden but the fight of two rams, and Caesar's thrasonical brag of "I came, saw, and overcame:" for your brother and my sister no sooner met but they looked; no sooner looked but they loved; no sooner loved but they sighed; no sooner sighed but they asked one another the reason; no sooner knew the reason but they sought the remedy: and in these degrees have they made a pair of stairs to marriage which they will climb incontinent, or

---

[1] *fair sister*] Rosalind is still disguised, and, as far as is known, Oliver believes her to be a boy. But he enters into Orlando's humour, and calls her "sister" in the spirit of Act IV, Sc. i. Cf. IV, iii, 86, where Oliver has already likened the boy Rosalind to "a ripe *sister.*"

[2] *in a scarf*] in a sling.

else be incontinent before marriage: they are in the very wrath of love and they will together; clubs cannot part them.

ORL.   They shall be married to-morrow, and I will bid the Duke to the nuptial.[3] But, O, how bitter a thing it is to look into happiness through another man's eyes! By so much the more shall I to-morrow be at the height of heart-heaviness, by how much I shall think my brother happy in having what he wishes for.

ROS.   Why then, to-morrow I cannot serve your turn for Rosalind?

ORL.   I can live no longer by thinking.

ROS.   I will weary you then no longer with idle talking. Know of me then, for now I speak to some purpose, that I know you are a gentleman of good conceit: I speak not this that you should bear a good opinion of my knowledge, insomuch I say I know you are; neither do I labour for a greater esteem than may in some little measure draw a belief from you, to do yourself good and not to grace me. Believe then, if you please, that I can do strange things: I have, since I was three year old, conversed with a magician, most profound in his art and yet not damnable. If you do love Rosalind so near the heart as your gesture cries it out, when your brother marries Aliena, shall you marry her: I know into what straits of fortune she is driven; and it is not impossible to me, if it appear not inconvenient to you, to set her before your eyes to-morrow human as she is and without any danger.

ORL.   Speakest thou in sober meanings?

ROS.   By my life, I do; which I tender dearly, though I say I am a magician.[4] Therefore, put you in your best array; bid your friends; for if you will be married to-morrow, you shall; and to Rosalind, if you will.

Enter SILVIUS *and* PHEBE

Look, here comes a lover of mine and a lover of hers.

PHE.   Youth, you have done me much ungentleness,
To show the letter that I writ to you.

ROS.   I care not if I have: it is my study
To seem despiteful and ungentle to you:
You are there followed by a faithful shepherd;
Look upon him, love him; he worships you.

PHE.   Good shepherd, tell this youth what 't is to love.

SIL.   It is to be all made of sighs and tears;

---

[3]*nuptial*] Shakespeare invariably uses the singular. The plural, "nuptials," is a more modern usage. Conversely he employs "funerals" where we use "funeral."

[4]*By my life . . . magician*] By statute law, 5 Eliz., Cap. 16, practisers of witchcraft were liable to punishment by death.

     And so am I for Phebe.

PHE.   And I for Ganymede.

ORL.   And I for Rosalind.

ROS.   And I for no woman.

SIL.   It is to be all made of faith and service;

     And so am I for Phebe.

PHE.   And I for Ganymede.

ORL.   And I for Rosalind.

ROS.   And I for no woman.

SIL.   It is to be all made of fantasy,

     All made of passion, and all made of wishes;

     All adoration, duty, and observance,[5]

     All humbleness, all patience, and impatience,

     All purity, all trial, all observance;

     And so am I for Phebe.

PHE.   And so am I for Ganymede.

ORL.   And so am I for Rosalind.

ROS.   And so am I for no woman.

PHE.   If this be so, why blame you me to love you?

SIL.   If this be so, why blame you me to love you?

ORL.   If this be so, why blame you me to love you?

ROS.   Why do you speak too, "Why blame you me to love you?"

ORL.   To her that is not here, nor doth not hear.

ROS.   Pray you, no more of this; 't is like the howling of Irish wolves against the moon.[6] [*To Sil.*] I will help you, if I can: [*To Phe.*] I would love you, if I could. To-morrow meet me all together. [*To Phe.*] I will marry you, if ever I marry woman, and I'll be married to-morrow: [*To Orl.*] I will satisfy you, if ever I satisfied man, and you shall be married to-morrow: [*To Sil.*] I will content you, if what pleases you contents you, and you shall be married to-morrow. [*To Orl.*] As you love Rosalind, meet: [*To Sil.*] as you love Phebe, meet: and as I love no woman, I'll meet. So, fare you well: I have left you commands.

SIL.   I'll not fail, if I live.

PHE.   Nor I.

ORL.   Nor I.   [*Exeunt.*

---

[5]*observance*] The repetition of this word at the end of the next line but one below suggests that one or other of the two "observances" is wrongly printed. The word seems somewhat more closely connected with "adoration" and "duty" as here, than with "purity" and "trial" as in line 91. Malone suggested *obedience* in the second place. Others prefer Ritson's conjecture of *obeisance*.

[6]*howling . . . moon*] Cf. Lodge's *Romance of Rosalynd*: "Thou barkest with the *wolves* of Syria *against the moone*." Wolves abounded in Ireland, and the substitution of the epithet *Irish* for *of Syria* is quite natural.

SCENE III. *The Forest.*

Enter TOUCHSTONE *and* AUDREY

TOUCH.   To-morrow is the joyful day, Audrey; to-morrow will we be
married.

AUD.   I do desire it with all my heart; and I hope it is no dishonest desire to desire to be a woman of the world.[1] Here come two of the
banished Duke's pages.

Enter two Pages

FIRST PAGE.   Well met, honest gentleman.

TOUCH.   By my troth, well met. Come, sit, sit, and a song.

SEC. PAGE.   We are for you: sit i' the middle.

FIRST PAGE.   Shall we clap into 't roundly,[2] without hawking or spit-
ting or saying we are hoarse, which are the only prologues to a bad
voice?

SEC. PAGE.   I' faith, i' faith; and both in a tune, like two gipsies on a
horse.

SONG

It was a lover and his lass,[3]
    With a hey, and a ho, and a hey nonino,
That o'er the green corn-field did pass
    In the spring time, the only pretty ring time,[4]

When birds do sing, hey ding a ding, ding:
Sweet lovers love the spring.

Between the acres of the rye,[5]
    With a hey, and a ho, and a hey nonino,
These pretty country folks would lie,
    In spring time, &c.

[1] *a woman of the world*] a married woman. Cf. *Much Ado*, II, i, 287. In *All's Well*, I, iii,
18, "To go *to the world*" means "to get married."
[2] *clap into 't roundly*] strike up the song straight away. Cf. *Much Ado*, III, iv, 38: "*Clap's*
into 'Light o' love.'"
[3] *seq. It was a lover, etc.*] The music of this song is found with the words in a volume of
MS. music in the Advocates' Library, Edinburgh, which seems to date from the early
part of the seventeenth century.
[4] *ring time*] The Folios read *rang time*, for which the Edinburgh MS. of the song substitutes *ring time, i.e.,* wedding time, which is obviously right.
[5] *Between the acres of the rye*] The reference seems to be to balks or banks of un-
ploughed turf which, in the common-field system of agriculture prevailing in
Elizabethan England, divided the acre strips of land from one another.

This carol they began that hour,
   With a hey, and a ho, and a hey nonino,
How that a life was but a flower
   In spring time, &c.

And therefore take the present time,
   With a hey, and a ho, and a hey nonino;
For love is crowned with the prime
   In spring time, &c.

TOUCH.   Truly, young gentlemen, though there was no great matter
   in the ditty, yet the note was very untuneable.[6]
FIRST PAGE.   You are deceived, sir: we kept time, we lost not our time.
TOUCH.   By my troth, yes; I count it but time lost to hear such a fool-
   ish song. God buy you;[7] and God mend your voices! Come,
   Audrey.   [Exeunt.

SCENE IV. *The Forest.*

Enter DUKE SENIOR, AMIENS, JAQUES, ORLANDO, OLIVER, *and* CELIA

DUKE S.   Dost thou believe, Orlando, that the boy
   Can do all this that he hath promised?
ORL.   I sometimes do believe, and sometimes do not;
   As those that fear they hope, and know they fear.[1]

Enter ROSALIND, SILVIUS, *and* PHEBE

ROS.   Patience once more, whiles our compact is urged:
   You say, if I bring in your Rosalind,
   You will bestow her on Orlando here?
DUKE S.   That would I, had I kingdoms to give with her.
ROS.   And you say, you will have her, when I bring her?

---

[6]*untuneable*] This is the reading of the Folios, for which Theobald substituted *untime-
able.* The change seems hardly necessary. "Out of *tune*" and "out of *time*" meant precisely the same thing.
[7]*God buy you*] God be with you. Cf. III, ii, 242.

[1]*fear they hope, and know they fear*] This, the original reading, has been often questioned, but no satisfactory substitute has been suggested. Orlando seeks to express the
extremity of his perplexity between hope and fear; he would seem to compare his lot
with those who have grave misgivings about what they hope, and their only sure knowledge is that they have misgivings.

ORL.   That would I, were I of all kingdoms king.
ROS.   You say, you'll marry me, if I be willing?
PHE.   That will I, should I die the hour after.
ROS.   But if you do refuse to marry me,
     You'll give yourself to this most faithful shepherd?
PHE.   So is the bargain.
ROS.   You say, that you'll have Phebe, if she will?
SIL.   Though to have her and death were both one thing.
ROS.   I have promised to make all this matter even.
     Keep you your word, O Duke, to give your daughter;
     You yours, Orlando, to receive his daughter:
     Keep your word, Phebe, that you'll marry me,
     Or else refusing me, to wed this shepherd:
     Keep your word, Silvius, that you'll marry her,
     If she refuse me: and from hence I go,
     To make these doubts all even.

                            [*Exeunt* ROSALIND *and* CELIA.

DUKE S.   I do remember in this shepherd boy
     Some lively touches of my daughter's favour.
ORL.   My lord, the first time that I ever saw him
     Methought he was a brother to your daughter:
     But, my good lord, this boy is forest-born,
     And hath been tutor'd in the rudiments
     Of many desperate studies by his uncle,
     Whom he reports to be a great magician,
     Obscured in the circle of this forest.

Enter TOUCHSTONE *and* AUDREY

JAQ.   There is, sure, another flood toward,[2] and these couples are com-
     ing to the ark. Here comes a pair of very strange beasts, which in
     all tongues are called fools.
TOUCH.   Salutation and greeting to you all!
JAQ.   Good my lord, bid him welcome: this is the motley-minded gen-
     tleman that I have so often met in the forest: he hath been a
     courtier, he swears.
TOUCH.   If any man doubt that, let him put me to my purgation. I
     have trod a measure; I have flattered a lady; I have been politic
     with my friend, smooth with mine enemy; I have undone three
     tailors; I have had four quarrels, and like to have fought one.
JAQ.   And how was that ta'en up?

---

[2]*toward*] imminent. Cf. *Hamlet*, V, ii, 356–357: "O proud death, What feast is *toward*
in thine eternal cell."

Touch.   Faith, we met, and found the quarrel was upon the seventh
    cause.[3]

Jaq.   How seventh cause? Good my lord, like this fellow.

Duke S.   I like him very well.

Touch.   God 'ild you,[4] sir; I desire you of the like. I press in here, sir,
    amongst the rest of the country copulatives, to swear and to for-
    swear; according as marriage binds and blood breaks: a poor vir-
    gin, sir, an ill-favoured thing, sir, but mine own; a poor humour of
    mine, sir, to take that that no man else will: rich honesty dwells
    like a miser, sir, in a poor house; as your pearl in your foul oyster.

Duke S.   By my faith, he is very swift and sententious.

Touch.   According to the fool's bolt, sir, and such dulcet diseases.[5]

Jaq.   But, for the seventh cause; how did you find the quarrel on the
    seventh cause?

Touch.   Upon a lie seven times removed:—bear your body more
    seeming, Audrey:—as thus, sir. I did dislike[6] the cut of a certain
    courtier's beard: he sent me word, if I said his beard was not cut
    well, he was in the mind it was: this is called the Retort Courteous.
    If I sent him word again "it was not well cut," he would send me
    word, he cut it to please himself: this is called the Quip Modest.
    If again "it was not well cut," he disabled my judgement: this is
    called the Reply Churlish. If again "it was not well cut," he would
    answer, I spake not true: this is called the Reproof Valiant. If again
    "it was not well cut," he would say, I lie: this is called the
    Countercheck Quarrelsome: and so to the Lie Circumstantial
    and the Lie Direct.

Jaq.   And how oft did you say his beard was not well cut?

Touch.   I durst go no further than the Lie Circumstantial, nor he
    durst not give me the Lie Direct; and so we measured swords and
    parted.

Jaq.   Can you nominate in order now the degrees of the lie?

[3]seventh cause] This is explained at line 65, infra, as "a lie seven times removed." The
duel ordinarily was caused by a quarrel in which one man gave the other the lie.
Touchstone distinguishes, infra, seven modes in which a lie may be given, ranging
from the "Retort Courteous" to the "Lie Direct." Shakespeare drew very literally this
account of such gradations of the lie from the popular handbook on the subject of
fencing and duelling by Vincent Saviolo, an Italian fencing master of London, whose
work, called "Vincentio Saviolo his Practise," was published in 1595.

[4]God 'ild you] God reward you. See footnote 8 on III, iii, 65, supra.

[5]dulcet diseases] Probably this is intentional nonsense with some such suggestion as
"charming disagreeablenesses." Johnson too seriously proposed to read discourses for
diseases.

[6]dislike] The word is often used, as here, not merely for entertaining, but also for expressing, dislike. Cf. Meas. for Meas., I, ii, 17: "I never heard any soldier dislike it."

TOUCH. O sir, we quarrel in print, by the book;[7] as you have books for
good manners:[8] I will name you the degrees. The first, the Retort
Courteous; the second, the Quip Modest; the third, the Reply
Churlish; the fourth, the Reproof Valiant; the fifth, the Counter-
check Quarrelsome; the sixth, the Lie with Circumstance; the seventh, the Lie Direct. All these you may avoid but the Lie Direct;
and you may avoid that too, with an If. I knew when seven justices
could not take up a quarrel, but when the parties were met themselves, one of them thought but of an If, as, "If you said so, then I
said so"; and they shook hands and swore brothers. Your If is the
only peace-maker; much virtue in If.

JAQ. Is not this a rare fellow, my lord? he's as good at any thing and
yet a fool.

DUKE S. He uses his folly like a stalking-horse[9] and under the pre-
sentation of that he shoots his wit.

Enter HYMEN, ROSALIND, *and* CELIA

Still Music

HYM.   Then is there mirth in heaven,
            When earthly things made even
                Atone together.
            Good Duke, receive thy daughter:
            Hymen from heaven brought her,
                Yea, brought her hither,
            That thou mightst join her hand[10] with his
            Whose heart within his bosom is.

ROS.   To you I give myself, for I am yours.
            To you I give myself, for I am yours.

DUKE S. If there be truth in sight, you are my daughter.

ORL.   If there be truth in sight, you are my Rosalind.

PHE.   If sight and shape be true,
            Why then, my love adieu!

ROS.   I'll have no father, if you be not he:
            I'll have no husband, if you be not he:
            Nor ne'er wed woman, if you be not she.

---

[7]*by the book*] An allusion probably to the book by Saviolo mentioned in footnote 3 on
line 49, *supra*.

[8]*books for good manners*] There were many such. Cf. Hugh Rhodes' *Boke of Nurture*,
or *Schole of good Manners* (1550?), and Sir Thomas Hoby's *The Courtyer* (1561).

[9]*stalking-horse*] Cf. Drayton's *Polyolbion*, Song 25: "One underneath his horse to get a
shoot doth *stalk*."

[10]*her hand*] This is the reading of the Third and Fourth Folios. The First and Second
Folios read *his hand*, obviously in error.

HYM.   Peace, ho! I bar confusion:
       'T is I must make conclusion
       Of these most strange events:
       Here's eight that must take hands
       To join in Hymen's bands,
         If truth holds true contents.
       You and you no cross shall part:
       You and you are heart in heart:
       You to his love must accord,
       Or have a woman to your lord:
       You and you are sure together,
       As the winter to foul weather.
       Whiles a wedlock-hymn we sing,
       Feed yourselves with questioning;
       That reason wonder may diminish,
       How thus we met, and these things finish.

SONG

       Wedding is great Juno's crown:
         O blessed bond of board and bed!
       'T is Hymen peoples every town;
         High wedlock then be honoured:
       Honour, high honour and renown,
       To Hymen, god of every town!

DUKE S.   O my dear niece, welcome thou art to me!
       Even daughter, welcome, in no less degree.
PHE.   I will not eat my word, now thou art mine;
       Thy faith my fancy to thee doth combine.

Enter JAQUES DE BOYS[11]

JAQ. DE B.   Let me have audience for a word or two:
       I am the second son of old Sir Rowland,
       That bring these tidings to this fair assembly.
       Duke Frederick, hearing how that every day
       Men of great worth resorted to this forest,
       Address'd a mighty power; which were on foot,
       In his own conduct, purposely to take
       His brother here and put him to the sword:
       And to the skirts of this wild wood he came;
       Where meeting with an old religious man,
       After some question with him, was converted
       Both from his enterprise and from the world;

---

[11]*Jaques de Boys*] See footnote 2 on I, i, 4.

His crown bequeathing to his banish'd brother,
And all their lands restored to them[12] again
That were with him exiled. This to be true,
I do engage my life.
DUKE S.   Welcome, young man;
Thou offer'st fairly to thy brothers' wedding:
To one his lands withheld; and to the other
A land itself at large, a potent dukedom.
First, in this forest let us do those ends
That here were well begun and well begot:
And after, every of this happy number,
That have endured shrewd[13] days and nights with us,
Shall share the good of our returned fortune,
According to the measure of their states.
Meantime, forget this new-fallen dignity,
And fall into our rustic revelry.
Play, music! And you, brides and bridegrooms all,
With measure heap'd in joy, to the measures fall.
JAQ.   Sir, by your patience. If I heard you rightly,
The Duke hath put on a religious life
And thrown into neglect the pompous court?
JAQ. DE B.   He hath.
JAQ.   To him will I: out of these convertites
There is much matter to be heard and learn'd.
[*To Duke S.*] You to your former honour I bequeath;
Your patience and your virtue well deserves it:
[*To Orl.*] You to a love, that your true faith doth merit:
[*To Oli.*] You to your land, and love, and great allies:
[*To Sil.*] You to a long and well-deserved bed:
[*To Touch.*] And you to wrangling; for thy loving voyage
Is but for two months victuall'd. So, to your pleasures:
I am for other than for dancing measures.
DUKE S.   Stay, Jaques, stay.
JAQ.   To see no pastime I: what you would have
I'll stay to know at your abandon'd cave.   [*Exit.*
DUKE S.   Proceed, proceed: we will begin these rites,
As we do trust they'll end, in true delights.   [*A dance.*

---

[12]*them*] This is Rowe's correction of the original reading *him*.
[13]*shrewd*] evil, disastrous. Cf. *Merch. of Ven.*, III, ii, 246: "There are some *shrewd* contents in yon same paper."

EPILOGUE

ROS. It is not the fashion to see the lady the epilogue; but it is no
more unhandsome than to see the lord the prologue. If it be true
that good wine needs no bush,[1] 't is true that a good play needs no
epilogue: yet to good wine they do use good bushes; and good
plays prove the better by the help of good epilogues. What a case
am I in then, that am neither a good epilogue, nor cannot insinu-
ate with you in the behalf of a good play! I am not furnished like
a beggar, therefore to beg will not become me: my way is to conjure you; and I'll begin with the women. I charge you, O women,
for the love you bear to men, to like as much of this play as please
you: and I charge you, O men, for the love you bear to women,—
as I perceive by your simpering, none of you hates them,—that between you and the women the play may please. If I were a woman[2]
I would kiss as many of you as had beards that pleased me, com-
plexions that liked me and breaths that I defied not: and, I am
sure, as many as have good beards or good faces or sweet breaths
will, for my kind offer, when I make curtsy, bid me farewell.

[*Exeunt.*

---

[1]*bush*] It was customary for tavern-keepers and vintners to hang a *bush* of holly or ivy
outside their houses, usually attached to the signboard.
[2]*If I were a woman*] The part of Rosalind, according to the practice of the Elizabethan
stage, was played by a boy.

Study Guide

Text by
Michael Morrison
(Ph.D., CUNY)

Department of English
DeVry Institute
Woodbridge, New Jersey

Contents

**Each Scene includes List of Characters,
Summary, Analysis, Study Questions and
Answers, and Suggested Essay Topics.**

SECTION ONE

Introduction

The Life and Work of William Shakespeare

The details of William Shakespeare's life are sketchy, mostly mere surmise based upon court or other clerical records. His parents, John and Mary (Arden), were married about 1557; she was of the landed gentry, and he was a yeoman—a glover and commodities merchant. By 1568, John had risen through the ranks of town government and held the position of high bailiff, which was a position similar to mayor. William, the eldest son and the third of eight children, was born in 1564, probably on April 23, several days before his baptism on April 26 in Stratford-upon-Avon. Shakespeare is also believed to have died on the same date—April 23—in 1616.

It is believed that William attended the local grammar school in Stratford where his parents lived, and that he studied primarily Latin, rhetoric, logic, and literature. Shakespeare probably left school at age 15, which was the norm, to take a job, especially since this was the period of his father's financial difficulty. At age 18 (1582), William married Anne Hathaway, a local farmer's daughter who was eight years his senior. Their first daughter (Susanna) was born six months later (1583), and twins Judith and Hamnet were born in 1585.

Shakespeare's life can be divided into three periods: the first 20 years in Stratford, which include his schooling, early marriage, and fatherhood; the next 25 years as an actor and playwright in London; and the last five in retirement in Stratford where he enjoyed moderate wealth gained from his theatrical successes. The years linking the first two periods are marked by a lack of information about Shakespeare, and are often referred to as the "dark years."

At some point during the "dark years," Shakespeare began his career with a London theatrical company, perhaps in 1589, for he was already an actor and playwright of some note by 1592. Shakespeare apparently wrote and acted for numerous theatrical companies, including Pembroke's Men, and Strange's Men, which later became the Chamberlain's Men, with whom he remained for the rest of his career.

In 1592, the Plague closed the theaters for about two years, and Shakespeare turned to writing book-length narrative poetry. Most notable were *Venus and Adonis* and *The Rape of Lucrece*, both of which were dedicated to the Earl of Southampton, whom scholars accept as Shakespeare's friend and benefactor despite a lack of documentation. During this same period, Shakespeare was writing his sonnets, which are more likely signs of the time's fashion rather than actual love poems detailing any particular relationship. He returned to playwriting when theaters reopened in 1594, and did not continue to write poetry. His sonnets were published without his consent in 1609, shortly before his retirement.

Amid all of his success, Shakespeare suffered the loss of his only son, Hamnet, who died in 1596 at the age of 11. But Shakespeare's career continued unabated, and in London in 1599, he became one of the partners in the new Globe Theater, which was built by the Chamberlain's Men.

Shakespeare wrote very little after 1612, which was the year he completed *Henry VIII*. It was during a performance of this play in 1613 that the Globe caught fire and burned to the ground. Sometime between 1610 and 1613, Shakespeare returned to Stratford, where he owned a large house and property, to spend his remaining years with his family.

William Shakespeare died on April 23, 1616, and was buried two days later in the chancel of Holy Trinity Church, where he had been baptized exactly 52 years earlier. His literary legacy included 37 plays, 154 sonnets, and five major poems.

Incredibly, most of Shakespeare's plays had never been published in anything except pamphlet form, and were simply extant as acting scripts stored at the Globe. Theater scripts were not regarded as literary works of art, but only the basis for the performance. Plays were simply a popular form of entertainment for all layers of society in Shakespeare's time. Only the efforts of two of Shakespeare's company, John Heminges and Henry Condell, preserved his 36 plays (minus *Pericles*, the thirty-seventh).

Shakespeare's Language

Shakespeare's language can create a strong pang of intimidation, even fear, in a large number of modern-day readers. Fortunately, however, this need not be the case. All that is needed to master the art of reading Shakespeare is to practice the techniques of unraveling uncommonly-structured sentences and to become familiar with the poetic use of uncommon words. We must realize that during the 400-year span between Shakespeare's time and our own, both the way we live and speak has changed. Although most of his vocabulary is in use today, some of it is obsolete, and what may be most confusing is that some of his words are used today, but with slightly different or totally different meanings. On the stage, actors readily dissolve these language stumbling blocks. They study Shakespeare's dialogue and express it dramatically in word and in action so that its meaning is graphically enacted. If the reader studies Shakespeare's lines as an actor does, looking up and reflecting upon the meaning of unfamiliar words until the real voice is discovered, he or she will suddenly experience the excitement, the depth, and the sheer poetry of what these characters say.

Shakespeare's Sentences

In English, or any other language, the meaning of a sentence greatly depends upon where each word is placed in that sentence. "The child hurt the mother" and "The mother hurt the child" have opposite meanings, even though the words are the same, simply because the words are arranged differently. Because word position is so integral to English, the reader will find unfamiliar word arrangements confusing, even difficult to understand. Since Shakespeare's plays are poetic dramas, he often shifts from average word arrangements to the strikingly unusual so that the line will conform to the desired poetic rhythm. Often, too, Shakespeare employs unusual word order to afford a character his own specific style of speaking.

Today, English sentence structure follows a sequence of subject first, verb second, and an optional object third. Shakespeare, however, often places the verb before the subject, which reads, "Speaks he" rather than "He speaks." Solanio speaks with this inverted structure in *The Merchant of Venice* stating, "I should be still/ Plucking the grass to know where sits the wind" (Bevington edition, I, i, ll. 17–19), while today's standard English word order would have the clause at the end of this line read, "where the wind sits." "Wind" is the subject of this clause, and "sits" is the verb. Bassanio's words in Act Two also exemplify this inversion: "And in such eyes as ours appear not faults" (II, ii, l. 184). In our normal word order, we would say, "Faults do not appear in eyes such as ours," with "faults" as the subject in both Shakespeare's word order and ours.

Inversions like these are not troublesome, but when Shakespeare positions the predicate adjective or the object before the subject and verb, we are sometimes surprised. For example, rather than "I saw him," Shakespeare may use a structure such as "Him I saw." Similarly, "Cold the morning is" would be used for our "The morning is cold." Lady Macbeth demonstrates this inversion as she speaks of her husband: "Glamis thou art, and Cawdor, and shalt be/What thou art promised" (*Macbeth*, I, v, ll. 14–15). In current English word order, this quote would begin, "Thou art Glamis, and Cawdor."

In addition to inversions, Shakespeare purposefully keeps words apart that we generally keep together. To illustrate, consider Bassanio's humble admission in *The Merchant of Venice*: "I owe you much, and, like a wilful youth,/That which I owe is lost" (I, i, ll. 146–147). The phrase, "like a wilful youth," separates the regular sequence of "I owe you much" and "That which I owe is lost." To understand more clearly this type of passage, the reader could rearrange these word groups into our conventional order: I owe you much and I wasted what you gave me because I was young and impulsive. While these rearranged clauses will sound like normal English, and will be simpler to understand, they will no longer have the desired poetic rhythm, and the emphasis will now be on the wrong words.

As we read Shakespeare, we will find words that are separated by long, interruptive statements. Often subjects are separated from verbs, and verbs are separated from objects. These long interruptions can be used to give a character dimension or to add an element of suspense. For example, in *Romeo and Juliet*, Benvolio describes both Romeo's moodiness and his own sensitive and thoughtful nature:

> I, measuring his affections by my own,
> Which then most sought, where most might not be
> found,
> Being one too many by my weary self,
> Pursu'd my humour, not pursuing his,
> And gladly shunn'd who gladly fled from me.
> (I, i, ll. 126–130)

In this passage, the subject "I" is distanced from its verb "Pursu'd." The long interruption serves to provide information which is integral to the plot. Another example, taken from *Hamlet*, is the ghost, Hamlet's father, who describes Hamlet's uncle, Claudius, as

> . . . that incestuous, that adulterate beast,
> With witchcraft of his wit, with traitorous gifts—
> O wicked wit and gifts, that have the power
> So to seduce—won to his shameful lust
> The will of my most seeming virtuous queen.
> (I, v, ll. 43–47)

From this we learn that Prince Hamlet's mother is the victim of an evil seduction and deception. The delay between the subject, "beast," and the verb, "won," creates a moment of tension filled with the image of a cunning predator waiting for the right moment to spring into attack. This interruptive passage allows the play to unfold crucial information and thus to build the tension necessary to produce a riveting drama.

While at times these long delays are merely for decorative purposes, they are often used to narrate a particular situation or to enhance character development. As *Antony and Cleopatra* opens, an interruptive passage occurs in the first few lines. Although the delay is not lengthy, Philo's words vividly portray Antony's military prowess while they also reveal the immediate concern of the drama. Antony is distracted from his career and is now focused on Cleopatra:

>   . . . those goodly eyes,
> That o'er the files and musters of the war
> Have glow'd like plated Mars, now bend, now turn
> The office and devotion of their view
> Upon a tawny front. . . .   (I, i, ll. 2–6)

Whereas Shakespeare sometimes heaps detail upon detail, his sentences are often elliptical, that is, they omit words we expect in written English sentences. In fact, we often do this in our spoken conversations. For instance, we say, "You see that?" when we really mean, "Did you see that?" Reading poetry or listening to lyrics in music conditions us to supply the omitted words and it makes us more comfortable reading this type of dialogue. Consider one passage in *The Merchant of Venice* where Antonio's friends ask him why he seems so sad and Solanio tells Antonio, "Why, then you are in love" (I, i, l. 46). When Antonio denies this, Solanio responds, "Not in love neither?" (I, i, l. 47). The word "you" is omitted but understood despite the confusing double negative.

In addition to leaving out words, Shakespeare often uses intentionally vague language, a strategy which taxes the reader's attentiveness. In *Antony and Cleopatra*, Cleopatra, upset that Antony is leaving for Rome after learning that his wife died in battle, convinces him to stay in Egypt:

> Sir, you and I must part, but that's not it:
> Sir you and I have lov'd, but there's not it;
> That you know well, something it is I would—
> O, my oblivion is a very Antony,

And I am all forgotten.
(I, iii, ll. 87–91, emphasis added)

In line 89, " . . . something it is I would" suggests that there is something that she would want to say, do, or have done. The intentional vagueness leaves us, and certainly Antony, to wonder. Though this sort of writing may appear lackadaisical for all that it leaves out, here the vagueness functions to portray Cleopatra as rhetorically sophisticated. Similarly, when asked what thing a crocodile is (meaning Antony himself who is being compared to a crocodile), Antony slyly evades the question by giving a vague reply:

It is shap'd, sir, like itself, and it is as broad as it hath breadth. It is just so high as it is, and moves with it own organs. It lives by that which nourisheth it, and, the elements once out of it, it transmigrates. (II, vii, ll. 43–46)

This kind of evasiveness, or double-talk, occurs often in Shakespeare's writing and requires extra patience on the part of the reader.

Shakespeare's Words

As we read Shakespeare's plays, we will encounter uncommon words. Many of these words are not in use today. As *Romeo and Juliet* opens, we notice words like "shrift" (confession) and "holidame" (a holy relic). Words like these should be explained in notes to the text. Shakespeare also employs words which we still use, though with different meaning. For example, in *The Merchant of Venice*, "caskets" refer to small, decorative chests for holding jewels. However, modern readers may think of a large cask instead of the smaller, diminutive casket.

Another trouble modern readers will have with Shakespeare's English is with words that are still in use today, but which mean something different in Elizabethan use. In *The Merchant of Venice*, Shakespeare uses the word "straight" (as in "straight away") where we would say "immediately." Here, the modern reader is unlikely to carry away the wrong message, however, since the modern meaning will simply make no sense. In this case, textual notes will clarify a phrase's meaning. To cite another example, in *Romeo and Juliet*, after Mercutio dies, Romeo states that the "black fate on moe days doth depend" (emphasis added). In this case, "depend" really means "impend."

Shakespeare's Wordplay

All of Shakespeare's works exhibit his mastery of playing with language and with such variety that many people have authored entire books on this subject alone. Shakespeare's most frequently used types of wordplay are common: metaphors, similes, synecdoche and metonymy, personification, allusion, and puns. It is when Shakespeare violates the normal use of these devices, or rhetorical figures, that the language becomes confusing.

A metaphor is a comparison in which an object or idea is replaced by another object or idea with common attributes. For example, in *Macbeth*, a murderer tells Macbeth that Banquo has been murdered, as directed, but that his son, Fleance, escaped, having witnessed his father's murder. Fleance, now a threat to Macbeth, is described as a serpent:

> There the grown serpent lies, the worm that's fled
> Hath nature that in time will venom breed,
> No teeth for the present. (III, iv, ll. 29–31, emphasis added)

Similes, on the other hand, compare objects or ideas while using the words "like" or "as." In *Romeo and Juliet*, Romeo tells Juliet that "Love goes toward love as schoolboys from their books" (II, ii, l. 156). Such similes often give way to more involved comparisons, "extended similes." For example, Juliet tells Romeo:

> 'Tis almost morning, I would have thee gone,
> And yet no farther than a wonton's bird,
> That lets it hop a little from his hand
> Like a poor prisoner in his twisted gyves,
> And with silken thread plucks it back again,
> So loving-jealous of his liberty
> (II, ii, ll. 176–181, emphasis added)

An epic simile, a device borrowed from heroic poetry, is an extended simile that builds into an even more elaborate comparison. In *Macbeth*, Macbeth describes King Duncan's virtues with an angelic, celestial simile and then drives immediately into another simile that redirects us into a vision of warfare and destruction:

> . . . Besides this Duncan
> Hath borne his faculties so meek, hath been
> So clear in his great office, that his virtues
> Will plead like angels, trumpet-tongued, against
> The deep damnation of his taking-off;
> And pity, like a naked new-born babe,
> Striding the blast, or heaven's cherubim, horsed
> Upon the sightless couriers of the air,
> Shall blow the horrid deed in every eye,
> That tears shall drown the wind. . . .
> (I, vii, ll. 16–25, emphasis added)

Shakespeare employs other devices, like synecdoche and metonymy, to achieve "verbal economy," or using one or two words to express more than one thought. Synecdoche is a figure of speech using a part for the whole. An example of synecdoche is using the word boards to imply a stage. Boards are only a small part of the materials that make up a stage, however, the term boards has become a colloquial synonym for stage. Metonymy is a figure of speech using the name of one thing for that of another which it is associated. An example of metonymy is using crown to mean the king (as used in the sentence "These lands belong to the crown"). Since a crown is associated with or an attribute of the king, the word crown has become a metonymy for the king. It is important to understand that every metonymy is a synecdoche, but not every synecdoche is a metonymy. This rule is true because a metonymy must not only be a part of the root word, making a synecdoche, but also be a unique attribute of or associated with the root word.

Synecdoche and metonymy in Shakespeare's works is often very confusing to a new student because he creates uses for words that they usually do not perform. This technique is often complicated and yet very subtle, which makes it difficult for a new student to dissect and understand. An example of these devices in one of Shakespeare's plays can be found in *The Merchant of Venice*. In warning his daughter, Jessica, to ignore the Christian revelries in the streets below, Shylock says:

> Lock up my doors; and when you hear the drum
> And the vile squealing of the wry-necked fife,
> Clamber not you up to the casements then . . .
> (I, v, ll. 30–32)

The phrase of importance in this quote is "the wry-necked fife." When a reader examines this phrase it does not seem to make sense; a fife is a cylinder-shaped instrument, there is no part of it that can be called a neck. The phrase then must be taken to refer to the fife-player, who has to twist his or her neck to play the fife. Fife, therefore, is a synecdoche for fife-player, much as boards is for stage. The trouble with understanding this phrase is that "vile squealing" logically refers to the sound of the fife, not the fife-player, and the reader might be led to take fife as the instrument because of the parallel reference to "drum" in the previous line. The best solution to this quandary is that Shakespeare uses the word fife to refer to both the instrument and the player. Both the player and the instrument are needed to complete the wordplay in this phrase, which, though difficult to understand to new readers, cannot be seen as a flaw since Shakespeare manages to convey two meanings with one word. This remarkable example of synecdoche illuminates Shakespeare's mastery of "verbal economy."

Shakespeare also uses vivid and imagistic wordplay through personification, in which human capacities and behaviors are attributed to inanimate objects. Bassanio, in *The Merchant of Venice*, almost speechless when Portia promises to marry him and share all her worldly wealth, states "my blood speaks to you in my veins . . ." (III, ii, l. 176). How deeply he must feel since even his blood can speak. Similarly, Portia, learning of the penalty that Antonio must pay for defaulting on his debt, tells Salerio,

"There are some shrewd contents in yond same paper/That steals the color from Bassanio's cheek" (III, ii, ll. 243-244).

Another important facet of Shakespeare's rhetorical repertoire is his use of allusion. An allusion is a reference to another author or to an historical figure or event. Very often Shakespeare alludes to the heroes and heroines of Ovid's *Metamorphoses*. For example, in Cymbeline an entire room is decorated with images illustrating the stories from this classical work, and the heroine, Imogen, has been reading from this text. Similarly, in *Titus Andronicus*, characters not only read directly from the *Metamorphoses*, but a subplot re-enacts one of the *Metamorphoses'* most famous stories, the rape and mutilation of Philomel.

Another way Shakespeare uses allusion is to drop names of mythological, historical, and literary figures. In *The Taming of the Shrew*, for instance, Petruchio compares Katharina, the woman whom he is courting, to Diana (II, i, l. 55), the virgin goddess, in order to suggest that Katharina is a man-hater. At times, Shakespeare will allude to well-known figures without so much as mentioning their names. In *Twelfth Night*, for example, though the Duke and Valentine are ostensibly interested in Olivia, a rich countess, Shakespeare asks his audience to compare the Duke's emotional turmoil to the plight of Acteon, whom the goddess Diana transforms into a deer to be hunted and killed by Acteon's own dogs:

Duke: That instant was I turn'd into a hart, And my
        desires, like fell and cruel hounds, E'er since
        pursue me. [. . .]
Valentine: But like a cloistress she will veiled walk,
            And water once a day her chamber round. . . .
            (I, i, l. 20 ff.)

Shakespeare's use of puns spotlights his exceptional wit. His comedies in particular are loaded with puns, usually of a sexual nature. Puns work through the ambiguity that results when multiple senses of a word are evoked; homophones often cause this sort of ambiguity. In *Antony and Cleopatra*, Enobarbus believes "there is mettle in death" (I, ii, l. 146), meaning that there is "courage" in death; at the same time, mettle suggests the homophone metal, referring to swords made of metal causing death. In early editions of Shakespeare's work there was no distinction made between the two words. Antony puns on the word "earing," (I, ii, ll. 112–114) meaning both plowing (as in rooting out weeds) and hearing: he angrily sends away a messenger, not wishing to hear the message from his wife, Fulvia: " . . . O then we bring forth weeds,/when our quick minds lie still, and our ills told us/Is as our earing." If ill-natured news is planted in one's "hearing," it will render an "earing" (harvest) of ill-natured thoughts. A particularly clever pun, also in *Antony and Cleopatra*, stands out after Antony's troops have fought Octavius's men in Egypt: "We have beat him to his camp. Run one before,/And let the queen know of our gests" (IV, viii, ll. 1–2). Here "gests" means deeds (in this case, deeds of battle); it is also a pun on "guests," as though Octavius' slain soldiers were to be guests when buried in Egypt.

One should note that Elizabethan pronunciation was in several cases different from our own. Thus, modern readers, especially Americans, will miss out on the many puns based on homophones. The textual notes will point out many of these "lost" puns, however.

Shakespeare's sexual innuendoes can be either clever or tedious depending upon the speaker and situation. The modern reader should recall that sexuality in Shakespeare's time was far more complex than in ours and that characters may refer to such things as masturbation and homosexual activity. Textual notes in some editions will point out these puns but rarely explain them. An example of a sexual pun or innuendo can be found in *The Merchant of Venice* when Portia and Nerissa are discussing Portia's past suitors using innuendo to tell of their sexual prowess:

Portia: I pray thee, overname them, and as thou
             namest them, I will describe them, and
             according to my description level at my
             affection.
Nerissa: First, there is the Neapolitan prince.
Portia: Ay, that's a colt indeed, for he doth nothing
             but talk of his horse, and he makes it a great

> appropriation to his own good parts that he
> can shoe him himself. I am much afeard my
> lady his mother played false with the smith.
> (I, ii, ll. 35–45)

The "Neapolitan prince" is given a grade of an inexperienced youth when Portia describes him as a "colt." The prince is thought to be inexperienced because he did nothing but "talk of his horse" (a pun for his penis) and his other great attributes. Portia goes on to say that the prince boasted that he could "shoe him [his horse] himself," a possible pun meaning that the prince was very proud that he could masturbate. Finally, Portia makes an attack upon the prince's mother, saying that "my lady his mother played false with the smith," a pun to say his mother must have committed adultery with a blacksmith to give birth to such a vulgar man having an obsession with "shoeing his horse."

It is worth mentioning that Shakespeare gives the reader hints when his characters might be using puns and innuendoes. In *The Merchant of Venice*, Portia's lines are given in prose when she is joking, or engaged in bawdy conversations. Later on the reader will notice that Portia's lines are rhymed in poetry, such as when she is talking in court or to Bassanio. This is Shakespeare's way of letting the reader know when Portia is jesting and when she is serious.

Shakespeare's Dramatic Verse

Finally, the reader will notice that some lines are actually rhymed verse while others are in verse without rhyme; and much of Shakespeare's drama is in prose. Shakespeare usually has his lovers speak in the language of love poetry which uses rhymed couplets. The archetypal example of this comes, of course, from *Romeo and Juliet*:

> The grey-ey'd morn smiles on the frowning night,
> Check'ring the eastern clouds with streaks of light,
> And fleckled darkness like a drunkard reels
> From forth day's path and Titan's fiery wheels.
> (II, iii, ll. 1–4)

Here it is ironic that Friar Lawrence should speak these lines since he is not the one in love. He, therefore, appears buffoonish and out of touch with reality. Shakespeare often has his characters speak in rhymed verse to let the reader know that the character is acting in jest, and vice-versa.

Perhaps the majority of Shakespeare's lines are in blank verse, a form of poetry which does not use rhyme (hence the name blank) but still employs a rhythm native to the English language, iambic pentameter, where every second syllable in a line of ten syllables receives stress. Consider the following verses from *Hamlet*, and note the accents and the lack of end-rhyme:

> The síngle ánd pecúliar lífe is bóund
> With áll the stréngth and ármor óf the mínd
> (III, iii, ll. 12–13)

The final syllable of these verses receives stress and is said to have a hard, or "strong," ending. A soft ending, also said to be "weak," receives no stress. In *The Tempest*, Shakespeare uses a soft ending to shape a verse that demonstrates through both sound (meter) and sense the capacity of the feminine to propagate:

> and thén I lóv'd thee
> And shów'd thee áll the quálitíes o' th' ísle,
> The frésh spríngs, bríne-pits, bárren pláce and fértile.
> (I, ii, ll. 338–40)

The first and third of these lines here have soft endings.

In general, Shakespeare saves blank verse for his characters of noble birth. Therefore, it is significant when his lofty characters speak in prose. Prose holds a special place in Shakespeare's dialogues; he uses it to represent the speech habits of the common people. Not only do lowly servants and common citizens speak in prose, but important, lower class figures also use this fun, at times ribald, variety of speech. Though Shakespeare crafts some very ornate lines in verse, his prose can be equally daunting, for some of his characters may speechify and break into double-talk in their attempts to show sophistication. A clever instance of this comes when the Third Citizen in *Coriolanus* refers to the people's paradoxical lack of power when they must elect Coriolanus as their new leader once Coriolanus has orated how he has courageously fought for them in battle:

> We have power in ourselves to do it, but
> it is a power that we have no power to do; for if he show us
> his wounds and tell us his deeds, we are to put our tongues
> into those wounds and speak for them; so, if he tell us his
> noble deeds, we must also tell him our noble acceptance of
> them. Ingratitude is monstrous, and for the multitude to
> be ingrateful were to make a monster of the multitude, of
> the which we, being members, should bring ourselves to be
> monstrous members.
> (II, ii, ll. 3–13)

Notice that this passage contains as many metaphors, hideous though they be, as any other passage in Shakespeare's dramatic verse.

When reading Shakespeare, paying attention to characters who suddenly break into rhymed verse, or who slip into prose after speaking in blank verse, will heighten your awareness of a character's mood and personal development. For instance, in *Antony and Cleopatra*, the famous military leader Marcus Antony usually speaks in blank verse, but also speaks in fits of prose (II, iii, ll. 43–46) once his masculinity and authority have been questioned. Similarly, in *Timon of Athens*, after the wealthy Lord Timon abandons the city of Athens to live in a cave, he harangues anyone whom he encounters in prose (IV, iii, l. 331 ff.). In contrast, the reader should wonder why the bestial Caliban in *The Tempest* speaks in blank verse rather than in prose.

Implied Stage Action

When we read a Shakespearean play, we are reading a performance text. Actors interact through dialogue, but at the same time these actors cry, gesticulate, throw tantrums, pick up daggers, and compulsively wash murderous "blood" from their hands. Some of the action that takes place on stage is explicitly stated in stage directions. However, some of the stage activity is couched within the dialogue itself. Attentiveness to these cues is important as one conceives how to visualize the action. When Iago in *Othello* feigns concern for Cassio whom he himself has stabbed, he calls to the surrounding men, "Come, come:/Lend me a light" (V, i, ll. 86–87). It is almost sure that one of the actors involved will bring him a torch or lantern. In the same play, Emilia, Desdemona's maidservant, asks if she should fetch her lady's nightgown and Desdemona replies, "No, unpin me here" (IV, iii, l. 37). In *Macbeth*, after killing Duncan, Macbeth brings the murder weapon back with him. When he tells his wife that he cannot return to the scene and place the daggers to suggest that the king's guards murdered Duncan, she castigates him: "Infirm of purpose/Give me the daggers. The sleeping and the dead are but as pictures" (II, ii, ll. 50–52). As she exits, it is easy to visualize Lady Macbeth grabbing the daggers from her husband.

For 400 years, readers have found it greatly satisfying to work with all aspects of Shakespeare's language—the implied stage action, word choice, sentence structure, and wordplay—until all aspects come to life. Just as seeing a fine performance of a Shakespearean play is exciting, staging the play in one's own mind's eye, and revisiting lines to enrich the sense of the action, will enhance one's appreciation of Shakespeare's extraordinary literary and dramatic achievements.

Historical Background

As You Like It was probably written in 1599 or 1600, at the midway point of Shakespeare's career as a playwright. His principal source for the play was Thomas Lodge's pastoral romance, *Rosalynde*. Lodge's novel, published in 1590, was in turn adapted from *The Tale of Gamelyn*, a 14th-century narrative poem. Shakespeare rewrote the story even further; he introduced new themes and created a number of new characters including Jaques, Touchstone, William, and Audrey. He also gave his characters far more depth and dimension than they had in Lodge's novel and added humor to the storyline.

Pastoral romance—a romantic story that takes place in a

rural or forest setting—was a popular category of literature and drama in Shakespeare's time. Love stories of innocent shepherds and shepherdesses and tales of woodland adventure were then in vogue. Shakespeare, a practical man of the theatre, created a play that he knew would appeal to his audience. The wrestling scene and the clowning of the rustic shepherds would have captured the attention of the groundlings, while the sophisticated wordplay would have impressed educated playgoers in the galleries. George Bernard Shaw felt that Shakespeare, in calling the play *As You Like It*, was commenting disparagingly on standards of contemporary theatrical taste. Yet it seems unlikely that Shakespeare had purely commercial considerations in mind when he wrote this play, for *As You Like It* does not adhere strictly to the conventions of pastoral romance. It satirizes them as well. The Forest of Arden is in many ways an idealized, fairy tale setting for the play, but it is also a place where "winter and rough weather" present hardships and wild beasts lurk as a threat. Shaw may have been correct, however, in his observation that Shakespeare was losing interest in crowd-pleasing comedies. Soon after he wrote *As You Like It*, Shakespeare abandoned comedy and turned to the composition of his major tragedies.

According to theatrical legend, Shakespeare—an actor as well as a playwright—played the old servant, Adam, when the play was presented by the Lord Chamberlain's Men (later the King's Men), the acting company of which he was a member. We have evidence that suggests this play was performed before King James I in 1603. In all likelihood it remained in the repertory of Shakespeare's company for a number of years after it was written.

As You Like It, although neglected in performance for more than a century after Shakespeare's death in 1616, has been a popular play on the stage ever since. It was revived in England for the first time in 1723 in an adaptation called *Love In A Forest*. This version of the play interpolated passages from other Shakespearean dramas and comedies, notably *A Midsummer Night's Dream*. Shakespeare's original was restored to the theatre seventeen years later. In the 19th century *As You Like It* was staged by a number of eminent English actor-managers including Charles

Kean and William Charles Macready. In late nineteenth century America, especially, the play became a favorite with audiences. Rosalind found noteworthy interpreters in Helena Modjeska, Mary Anderson, Ada Rehan, and Julia Marlowe.

More recently, the role of Rosalind has attracted a number of leading actresses including Peggy Ashcroft, Katharine Hepburn, and Vanessa Redgrave. In 1967, the National Theatre of Great Britain staged an all-male production of the play, and in 1991 England's experimental Cheek By Jowl company mounted a similar production. Thus, modern audiences were introduced to a theatrical convention of Shakespeare's time, when young men played all the women's roles. Both productions were well received by audiences and critics and subsequently toured the United States. Also noteworthy is the Renaissance Theatre Company's 1988 Edwardian dress production in London with Kenneth Branagh as Touchstone. Today, when there are more than three hundred Shakespeare festivals worldwide, *As You Like It* remains one of the Bard's most well-loved and frequently produced comedies.

Master List of Characters

Duke Senior—*An exiled Duke, living in banishment in the Forest of Arden.*

Duke Frederick—*Duke Senior's brother; usurper of his dukedom.*

Amiens—*A courtier and singer who attends Duke Senior in exile.*

First and Second Lords—*Courtiers who attend Duke Senior in exile.*

Jaques—*A melancholy philosopher who resides with the exiled Duke Senior in the Forest of Arden.*

Le Beau—*A foppish courtier attending Duke Frederick.*

Charles—*A wrestler at the court of Duke Frederick.*

Oliver—*Eldest son of the late Sir Rowland de Boys and heir to his father's estate.*

Jaques de Boys—*The middle son of the late Sir Rowland de Boys.*

Orlando—*Youngest son of the late Sir Rowland de Boys who falls in love with Rosalind.*

Adam—*A loyal, elderly servant in the household of the late Sir Rowland de Boys who accompanies Orlando to the Forest of Arden.*

Dennis—*Another servant in the household of the late Sir Rowland de Boys.*

Touchstone—*A clown at the court of Duke Frederick who accompanies Rosalind and Celia into exile.*

Sir Oliver Martext—*A clergyman.*

Corin—*An old shepherd who lives near the Forest of Arden.*

Silvius—*A young, lovelorn shepherd.*

William—*A simpleminded young man.*

Hymen—*The god of marriage.*

Rosalind—*Daughter of the banished Duke Senior who falls in love with Orlando.*

Celia—*Rosalind's loyal friend and daughter of Duke Frederick.*

Phebe—*A shepherdess.*

Audrey—*A country wench.*

Summary of the Play

Orlando, youngest son of the late Sir Rowland de Boys, complains to Adam, an elderly family servant, that his brother Oliver has unfairly withheld his late father's inheritance and prevented him from being educated as a gentleman. Oliver enters and a heated argument ensues. When Oliver learns that his brother plans to challenge Charles, Duke Frederick's hulking wrestler, he plots with Charles to break his brother's neck during the match.

The next day Duke Frederick, his daughter Celia, and his niece Rosalind witness the competition. Charles has subdued his first three opponents, but Orlando manages to defeat his adversary. Duke Frederick is infuriated when he learns the identity of Orlando's father, in life his bitter enemy, but Rosalind is captivated by Orlando and gives him a chain from her neck as a reward for his victory. Orlando is immediately taken by her charm, yet he finds himself speechless to thank her.

Rosalind, daughter of the banished Duke Senior whom Frederick has usurped, tells Celia that she has fallen in love with Orlando. Duke Frederick has allowed Rosalind to remain at court because of her friendship with his daughter, but now he banishes her, despite Celia's pleas to allow her to remain. Rosalind and Celia make plans to join Rosalind's father in the Forest of Arden. They decide to travel in disguise, Rosalind as Ganymede, a young man, and Celia as Aliena, a peasant girl. Touchstone, Duke Frederick's court jester, agrees to accompany them.

Duke Frederick is enraged when he learns that his daughter and Rosalind have fled. He believes Orlando is with them and plans a search party, led by Oliver, to find them. Orlando, meanwhile, has learned from Adam that Oliver is plotting to have him killed and they make plans to leave the court for the countryside.

Rosalind and Celia, now in disguise, arrive in the Forest of Arden along with Touchstone. There they overhear a young shepherd, Silvius, tell an old Shepherd, Corin, of his love for Phebe, a shepherdess who has spurned his affections. Orlando and Adam, in the meantime, have arrived in another part of the forest. Adam becomes weak with hunger and Orlando sets out in search of food. He soon discovers the banished Duke Senior and his court and confronts them with his sword drawn. Duke Senior greets him with kindness, however, and invites him to share in his feast. Orlando agrees and leaves to bring Adam to safety.

Obsessed by his love for Rosalind, Orlando writes poems about her and hangs them on trees. Rosalind discovers the poems and is critical of their literary merit, but when she learns they are by Orlando, she has a change of heart. She meets Orlando, who does not recognize her in her male disguise, and offers to cure him of his lovesickness if he will court her as if she were Rosalind. Touchstone, in the meantime, has begun courting Audrey, a goatherd, and Silvius has continued to pursue the shepherdess he loves. Phebe, however, has fallen in love with Rosalind in her Ganymede disguise.

Orlando meets with Rosalind and tells her how he would charm and win his beloved. Oliver arrives in the forest soon afterward and tells Rosalind and Celia that Orlando, unaware of

Oliver's identity, had rescued him from a lioness while he slept beneath a tree. He tells them he is Orlando's brother, and that he and Orlando have reconciled. When he reveals that Orlando was wounded by the lioness, Rosalind faints.

Oliver confesses to Orlando that he has fallen in love with Celia. Orlando tells Rosalind that his brother's marriage is to take place the next day and wishes he could marry his own beloved. Rosalind, still in disguise, tells him that through "magic" she will make her appear. She also pledges to help Silvius and Phebe. Touchstone tells Audrey that they, too, will be married on the morrow.

The next day, Rosalind reveals her true identity and she and Orlando, Oliver and Celia, and Silvius and Phebe are married before the banished Duke. Jaques de Boys, the middle son of Sir Rowland, brings the news that Duke Frederick has met an old religious hermit and has decided to forsake the world and restore his brother's dukedom. The newly united couples dance and Rosalind speaks the epilogue.

Estimated Reading Time

This play should take the average student about five hours to read. It will be helpful to divide your reading time into five one-hour sittings for each of the play's five acts. Shakespeare's language can be difficult for students who are unfamiliar with it, so each act should be read carefully on a scene by scene basis to ensure understanding.

SECTION TWO

Act I

Act I, Scene I (pages 1–5)

New Characters:

Orlando: *youngest son of the late Sir Rowland de Boys*

Adam: *an elderly servant in the household of the late Rowland de Boys*

Dennis: *another servant in the household*

Oliver: *eldest son of the late Sir Rowland de Boys and inheritor of his father's estate*

Charles: *Duke Frederick's wrestler*

Summary

Scene I, set in the orchard of the de Boys family, begins with the entrance of Orlando de Boys and Adam, an elderly servant. Orlando complains to Adam that his late father had bequeathed him a thousand crowns and requested that his oldest brother Oliver provide for his education as a gentleman. Although Oliver has kept the second brother of the family at school, he has treated his youngest brother no better than one of his horses or oxen and has refused to honor his father's will.

Oliver enters and a violent quarrel ensues as Orlando confronts his brother with his resentment. Oliver strikes Orlando, but Orlando puts a wrestler's grip on his brother and subdues him. Adam parts the brothers and Orlando asks for his rightful inheritance. Oliver dismisses them harshly. After Orlando and Adam leave, Dennis, a servant, enters and tells Oliver that Charles, Duke Frederick's wrestler, has come to speak with him. Charles brings the news that the old Duke Senior has been banished by his younger brother, Duke Frederick, who has usurped his title and lands. The old Duke and his lords have gone into exile in the nearby Forest of Arden where they are living like Robin Hood and his Merry Men. Rosalind, the old Duke's daughter, has been allowed to remain at court as the result of her friendship with Celia, Duke Frederick's daughter.

Charles tells Oliver that he plans to wrestle the next day before Duke Frederick and has learned that Orlando plans to challenge him. He urges Oliver to tell Orlando to withdraw from the match to avoid bodily harm. Oliver assures Charles that his brother is "a secret and villainous contriver" against his "natural brother" and tells him "I had as lief thou didst break his neck as his finger" during the match. He warns Charles that Orlando might resort to treachery to defeat him. After Charles exits, Oliver confesses that he hates and envies Orlando and hopes the match will bring "an end" to his brother.

Analysis

In Medieval and Renaissance Europe, a system existed known as primogeniture. The land, money, and goods owned by a family often passed by law or by sanctioned custom into the hands of the family's eldest son, to the exclusion of other family members. Thus, Oliver would not have been legally bound (or bound by the customs of the time) to honor the terms of his father's bequests to Orlando. He had a moral obligation, of course, but chose to ignore it.

By establishing Orlando immediately as a young man who has been wronged, Shakespeare engages our sympathy for this character. Even his brother later confesses that he's "gentle . . . full of noble device, of all sorts enchantingly beloved." Oliver, on the other hand, is established as an unjust and treacherous character who has deliberately ignored his late father's bequest of money and his wish that he provide for Orlando's education as a gentleman. We also learn that he is willing to resort to dishonest means to see his brother out of the way.

The relationship between Oliver and Orlando is paralleled by the relationship between Duke Frederick and the deposed Duke Senior. In both instances, a brother has been treated unfairly. There is one noteworthy difference, however. Duke Senior is the elder brother and rightful heir to the dukedom. Duke Frederick's usurpation is both immoral and unlawful.

When we learn that Duke Senior and his court-in-exile "fleet the time carelessly as they did in the golden world" we are introduced to one of the play's many themes: the issue of city life versus country life. The court—and the de Boys household—are characterized by animosity and malice, whereas Duke Senior's pastoral existence in the Forest of Arden is idealized.

Act I, Scenes II and III (pages 5–16)

New Characters:

Rosalind: *daughter of the exiled Duke Senior*

Celia: *daughter of Duke Frederick and Rosalind's loyal friend*

Touchstone: *Duke Frederick's court jester*

Le Beau: *a foppish courtier*

Duke Frederick: *usurper of his brother's dukedom; Celia's father and Rosalind's uncle*

Summary

The next day, Rosalind, daughter of the banished Duke Senior, and Celia, Duke Frederick's daughter, are encountered at Duke Frederick's palace. Celia urges her cousin to "be merry," but Rosalind is still upset by her father's banishment. Celia attempts to cheer her up by pledging her friendship and affection. Rosalind agrees to be joyful for her sake, and to "devise sports." She asks Celia what she would think of falling in love, to which Celia replies that love is best treated as a "sport" rather than in earnest. The young women banter lightheartedly about the caprices of "fortune" and "nature." Touchstone, Duke Frederick's court jester, arrives on the scene. He engages in witty chatter and tells Celia that her father has summoned her. Le

Beau, one of Duke Frederick's courtiers, enters and informs Rosalind and Celia that the wrestling matches are underway. Charles has defeated his first three challengers, doing bodily harm in the process.

Duke Frederick and his court, along with Orlando and Charles, arrive for the next match. Duke Frederick is worried for Orlando's safety and urges his daughter and niece to dissuade him from competing. Their attempts are met by Orlando's firm declaration that "If killed . . . I shall do my friends no wrong for I have none to lament me; the world no injury, for in it I have nothing." The match begins and Rosalind and Celia cheer for Orlando. Then, to the astonishment of the onlookers, Orlando throws his opponent. Duke Frederick orders the match to a halt. Orlando wants to continue, but Charles is vanquished and is carried off.

Duke Frederick inquires of the victor's name, but when he learns that Orlando is the son of the late Sir Rowland de Boys, an ally of the banished Duke, his manner becomes harsh. "I would thou hadst been son to some man else," he remarks. Although the world esteemed Sir Rowland as honorable, Frederick considered him an enemy. He exits with his court. Rosalind and Celia remain.

Orlando proclaims that he is proud to have been Sir Rowland's son and Rosalind comments that her father "lov'd Sir Rowland as his soul." She gives Orlando a chain from around her neck, but Orlando, who has fallen in love at first sight, is speechless and unable to thank her. Rosalind and Celia exit and Le Beau warns Orlando that the Duke is furious at his victory. He advises him to "leave this place" and also tells him that the Duke has recently "ta'en displeasure 'gainst his gentle niece" since the people "praise her for her virtues" and "pity her for her father's sake." Le Beau exits and Orlando, alone, notes that he must now go from facing "a tyrant Duke" to facing a "tyrant brother." Yet at the same time he has something to cheer his spirits: "heavenly Rosalind."

In Scene III, also set at Duke Frederick's palace, Rosalind confesses to Celia that she has fallen in love with Orlando. Their conversation grinds to a halt, however, when Duke Frederick enters "with his eyes full of anger" and banishes Rosalind from the court. When Rosalind asks for an explanation she is told, "Thou art thy father's daughter, there's enough." Celia pleads with her father for Rosalind to remain, but the Duke refuses. Celia tells him that if Rosalind is banished she will go as well. Duke Frederick calls her a fool and exits.

Celia suggests that they join Rosalind's father in the Forest of Arden. Rosalind protests that the journey will be dangerous for young women: "Beauty provoketh thieves sooner than gold." Celia proposes that they travel in disguise and resolves to dress in peasant attire and call herself Aliena. Rosalind, the taller of the pair, decides to dress as a young man and call herself Ganymede. They make plans to lure Touchstone along for the journey to divert them. They exit to pack their "jewels" and "wealth" and view their flight from the court as a journey "to liberty, and not to banishment."

Analysis

The loyal friendship between Rosalind and Celia contrasts sharply with the antagonistic relationship between their fathers and that of Orlando and Oliver. Earlier, we have been told that they were "ever from their cradles bred together" and that "never two ladies loved as they do." Now we see their relationship first-hand. This continues a pattern of hearing about a relationship before it is shown on stage. In the first scene, for example, we heard of Oliver's unjust treatment of Orlando, then Oliver entered and confirmed his account. We already know that Duke Senior and his court are living in the forest of Arden like Robin Hood and his Merry Men; later we will see them doing just that.

Early in the second scene, Shakespeare introduces two additional themes: fortune and nature. Rosalind and Celia engage in witty wordplay in their discussion of these elements. Celia comments that fortune's gifts are not bestowed equally and Rosalind adds that the "goddess" fortune is, by tradition, blind. As we have seen, even those who are gifted by nature can suffer the caprices of fortune. Orlando, for example, is noble by nature, yet fortune has deprived him of his father's bequests. These thematic motifs will recur many times in the play. Later in this scene, for example, Rosalind, after giving Orlando her chain, describes herself as "one out of suits with fortune." This scene also introduces the theme of love, which will be explored in many of its aspects. In the opening exchange between Celia and Rosalind, the platonic love among cousins is contrasted with romantic love. Celia advises Rosalind to view romance as a "sport" but not in earnest. By the end of the scene, however, Rosalind will have fallen in love with Orlando. We also learn that Rosalind's father had loved Orlando's father "with all his soul."

The characters of Touchstone and Le Beau serve particular functions in *As You Like It*. Touchstone, a witty court fool, impudent, wise, shrewd, and verbally dextrous, has a special license to speak his mind freely. He comments on the action with subtle irony. When Rosalind and Celia are summoned to the wrestling match after Charles has injured three opponents, for instance, he remarks wryly that "It is the first time that ever I heard breaking of ribs was sport for ladies." In Shakespeare's time, a "touchstone" was the stone on which precious metals were rubbed to test their genuineness. The character of Touchstone similarly exposes the inner natures of those he meets. Le Beau, on the other hand, is revealed through his pompous speech and dandified dress as a character who is affected rather than "natural." He represents the formality of the court as opposed to the freer, more spontaneous life many of the characters will encounter in the Forest of Arden.

In Scene III, we learn that Rosalind's thoughts have now turned, in part, from her father to the future and her "child's father." As in the previous scene, Shakespeare uses clever wordplay that builds on a wrestling analogy: Celia urges Rosalind to "wrestle with her affections" and comments on her sudden "fall" into "so strong a liking" for Orlando.

Duke Frederick further reveals his villainous nature when he forces Rosalind into banishment as he had earlier banished her father. Celia demonstrates her loyalty to her cousin by resolving to accompany her. Their decision to travel in disguise has a practical purpose, for as Rosalind comments, it is dangerous for women to venture forth alone in the countryside. Her determination to travel in a man's apparel as Ganymede will help to assure their safety.

In classical mythology, Ganymede, a beautiful Trojan youth who was seized and carried to Mount Olympus by Zeus' eagle, was the cup bearer of the gods. By tradition, he was beloved by Zeus, the king of the gods (also known as Jupiter and Jove). When Rosalind declares, "I'll have no worse a name than Jove's own page," many in Shakespeare's audience would have known that this myth, with its connotations of same sex romantic love, would underscore the comic action of the play. This reference also foreshadows the appearance of a mythological god in the final scene.

Rosalind's new identity will also serve a purely dramatic purpose. Disguise was an essential convention of Elizabethan drama and Shakespeare's plays in particular. This device will later prove to be an important element of the plot. Many of the complications in the acts that follow will result from other characters believing that Rosalind is a young man. Thus, the audience (or the reader) is in on a secret that many characters in the play will not know.

With Celia's declaration in the concluding line that the young women are going "to liberty, and not to banishment," Shakespeare again contrasts city life and pastoral life. The court, as we have seen, is a place of tyranny and corruption, yet the Forest of Arden, although not without its perils, will be revealed mainly as an idyllic green world of harmony and understanding.

Study Questions

1. Why does Orlando resent the way he has been treated by his brother Oliver?

2. How does Charles describe the exiled Duke Senior and his court?

3. Why does Duke Frederick allow the daughter of his banished brother to remain at court?

4. What plot does Oliver hatch against Orlando?

5. Why is Orlando warned not to wrestle with Charles?

6. What gift does Rosalind give to Orlando after he wins his wrestling match?

7. How do we know that Rosalind and Orlando have fallen in love at first sight?

8. What warning does Le Beau bring to Orlando after the match?

9. What are the reasons Duke Frederick gives for banishing Rosalind?

10. Why do Rosalind and Celia disguise themselves when they leave the court?

Answers

1. Orlando resents his treatment at his brother's hands because Oliver has ignored the bequests made by their late father. Sir Rowland de Boys left Orlando a thousand crowns and requested that Oliver provide for his education as a gentleman, but Oliver has kept Orlando "rustically at home" and has treated him no better than one of his horses or oxen.

2. Charles describes the exiled Duke and his court as living like Robin Hood and his Merry Men in the Forest of Arden. There they "fleet the time carelessly as they did in the golden world."

3. Duke Frederick has allowed Rosalind to remain at court because of her friendship with his daughter Celia. Charles tells Oliver that "the Duke's daughter her cousin so loves her, being ever from their cradles bred together, that she would have followed her exile, or have died to stay behind her."

4. Oliver plots to have Charles disable or kill Orlando during the wrestling match scheduled for the next day. He tells Charles "I had as lief thou didst break his neck as his finger" and warns him that Orlando may resort to poison or treachery if Charles does not take care of him first.

5. Celia, at Duke Frederick's bidding, warns Orlando that he has seen "cruel proof" of Charles's strength. Charles has seriously injured his first three opponents and Orlando's safety is at stake.

6. Rosalind gives Orlando a chain from around her neck and bids him to "wear this for me."

7. Rosalind tells Orlando, "Sir, you have wrestled well, and overthrown/ More than your enemies." After Rosalind exits, Orlando proclaims, "O poor Orlando, thou art overthrown!/ Or Charles, or something weaker master thee."

8. Le Beau tells Orlando to "leave this place" because the Duke is angry and there is no telling what he might do.

9. Duke Frederick accuses Rosalind of being a traitor and says he does not trust her. When asked to explain his reasoning he replies, "Thou art thy father's daughter, there's enough."

10. Rosalind and Celia decide to disguise themselves because it would be dangerous for young women to travel alone in the countryside.

Suggested Essay Topics

1. Discuss the concepts of fortune and nature as they apply to Orlando and Oliver.

2. Compare and contrast the relationship of Oliver and Orlando with that of Rosalind and Celia.

3. Explore the ways that Shakespeare uses witty wordplay based on "sport" and "wrestling" analogies to reveal his characters' views on the subject of love.

4. Compare the impressions we get of court life and country life in the first act.

SECTION THREE

Act II

Act II, Scene I (pages 17–19)

New Characters:

Duke Senior: *an exiled duke, living in banishment in the Forest of Arden; Rosalind's father and Celia's uncle*

Amiens: *a courtier and singer who attends Duke Senior*

First and Second Lords: *courtiers who attend Duke Senior in exile*

Summary

Scene I takes place in the Forest Arden. Duke Senior tells his "co-mates and brothers in exile" that he finds life in the forest "more sweet" and "free from peril" than life at "the envious court," despite the inconvenience of cold and winter winds. Amiens, one of the Duke's courtiers, agrees, noting that the Duke has turned the misfortune of his banishment into a happy life in the forest. Duke Senior proposes that he and his courtiers embark on a deer hunt, although he regrets having to kill deer "in their own confines." The First Lord replies that Jaques, another courtier, also feels remorse at having to kill animals for food. That day, Jaques had come upon a deer wounded by a hunter. This sight had moved him to tears and philosophical reflection. He had observed cynically that Duke Senior and his courtiers were usurpers and tyrants themselves for frightening and killing the animals in the forest. Duke Senior asks to be taken to the place where Jaques has remained, "weeping and commenting" upon the fallen deer, for he enjoys encountering Jaques when he is in one of his melancholy moods.

Analysis

In Scene I, we learn that Duke Senior, although banished from his dukedom and lands, has made the most of his misfortune. Duke Senior's comments on his existence in the Forest of Arden are yet another paean to the pastoral life. Here, we see a far more relaxed atmosphere than we have seen at court. We are in the presence of a new social order. Duke Senior and his court-in-exile have cast aside what is "painted" and "envious." We are also greeted by images of bountiful nature: in the forest, Duke Senior remarks, one can find "tongues in trees, books in the running brooks,/ Sermons in stones, and good in everything." Yet life in the forest, as we learn in Duke Senior's opening speech, also has its hazards, particularly the "icy fang" of the winter wind. Duke Senior is optimistic by nature, however, and he seems undiscouraged by the hardships he and his court have endured. When he mentions that "Here feel we not the penalty of Adam," he is comparing life in the Forest of Arden to man's idyllic existence in the Garden of Eden.

Our introduction to Jaques (pronounced "jay-kweez") continues the pattern of hearing about many of the principal characters before they appear in the play. We learn that Jaques, like Duke Senior, has qualms about killing deer for food. His reaction to this element of life in the forest is much more extreme than the Duke's. Encountering a deer wounded by a hunter's arrow has provoked one of his philosophical moods. Jaques's ironic observation that Duke Senior and his courtiers have usurped the rightful domain of the animals, just as Duke Frederick has usurped his brother's dukedom, has some validity. His pronouncements are reminders that the forest, like the court, is also home to pain and suffering.

Unlike the court, however, this society is a place where diverse types coexist in harmony. It is permissive haven for a misanthrope such as Jaques. Yet it is apparent that Duke Senior, while enjoying Jaques' company and savoring the entertainment he provides, does not take his philosophy seriously. As he remarks, "I love to cope him in these sullen fits,/ For then he's full of matter."

Act II, Scenes II and III (pages 19–22)

Summary

In Scene II, set at Duke Frederick's palace, Duke Frederick reveals his anger when he learns that Rosalind, Celia, and Touchstone are missing. A courtier tells him that Orlando is believed to be in their company. Duke Frederick orders Orlando to be summoned immediately, or for Oliver to be brought should Orlando be missing. If Orlando is gone, the Duke will make Oliver find his brother.

Scene III takes place at Oliver's house. Adam, in a state of agitation, warns Orlando that he is in mortal danger if he remains at home. Oliver has learned of Orlando's victory in the wrestling match, and he plans to burn Orlando's lodgings that very night while Orlando is sleeping. If that fails, Oliver will resort to other treacherous means to kill his brother. Orlando is uncertain as to where he might go, but Adam tells him that any place is better than remaining at home. Orlando protests that with no money of his own, his only options would be to "beg for food" or to make "a thievish living on the common road." Adam tells Orlando that he has saved five hundred crowns during his years of service to Orlando's late father, which he had set aside for his old age. He offers Orlando the money and begs to accompany him wherever he goes. Orlando, moved by Adam's loyalty, invites him to share his journey into exile.

Analysis

These brief scenes contrast the villainy of Duke Frederick and Oliver with the noble natures of Adam and Orlando. Adam is in many ways a model of virtue. From the age of seventeen "till now almost fourscore" he has served Sir Rowland de Boys and his household faithfully. He has managed to save five hundred crowns by leading an exemplary life. In his youth he avoided "hot and rebellious liquors" and other vices. Orlando comments admiringly that Adam is "not for the fashion of these times"—an allusion to the corruption of the court. Yet we can see that Orlando, too, is virtuous. The idea of earning his living as a beggar or a thief is so repugnant to him that he is willing to risk remaining at home. Here again, we see the theme of fortune when Adam tells Orlando at the end of Scene III, "Yet fortune cannot recompense me better/Than to die well and not my master's debtor."

Act II, Scene IV (pages 22–25)

New Characters

Corin: *an old shepherd who dwells near the Forest of Arden*

Silvius: *a young shepherd who is in love with Phebe, a shepherdess*

Summary

Rosalind and Celia, now disguised as Ganymede, a young man, and Aliena, a peasant girl, arrive in the Forest of Arden along with Touchstone. All three are weary in body and spirit after their long journey. As they rest, Corin, an old shepherd, and Silvius, a young shepherd, enter. Rosalind, Celia, and Touchstone overhear their conversation. Silvius sighs that he is hopelessly in love with Phebe, a disdainful shepherdess who has spurned his affections. Corin offers his advice. He assures Silvius that in his younger years, he, too, had been driven to madness by love. However Silvius refuses to believe that anyone could love as he does. He remarks that if Corin has never "broke from company/ Abruptly as my passion now makes me," he has never experienced love. Distraught, and true to his word, he runs off, calling Phebe's name. After he exits, Rosalind is reminded of her longing for Orlando, and Touchstone recalls one of his own youthful romantic adventures.

Celia, famished, asks Touchstone to inquire if Corin can provide them with food. Corin tells the visitors from the court that he is merely the hired shepherd of an uncharitable landowner and cannot grant their request. He adds, however, that the cottage, land, and sheep owned by the man whose herd he tends are for sale. Silvius is the intended buyer, but at present he is so obsessed by his love for Phebe that he "cares little for buying anything." Rosalind tells Corin to purchase the flock and property for her, and she promises to retain Corin as shepherd and raise his wages.

Analysis

Early in this scene, Rosalind proclaims: "Well, this is the Forest of Arden." This announcement would have served a practical purpose for Shakespeare's audience. The theatre of Shakespeare's time featured little or no scenery—a single tree may have sufficed for the entire forest. Thus, Rosalind's comment would have established the locale.

Rosalind and Celia have now adopted their disguises, in which they will remain until the last scene of the play. Rosalind comments early in this scene on the disparity between her outward appearance and her inner feelings: "I could find in my heart to disgrace my man's apparel and to cry like a woman." In Shakespeare's time, the role of Rosalind was portrayed by a young man. Elizabethan audiences would have appreciated the irony of a young man playing a young woman disguised as a man.

The young, lovelorn shepherd was one of the conventions of pastoral romance. Here we see a romantic infatuation similar to that felt by Rosalind and Orlando, yet Silvius' yearning for Phebe is more comically extravagant. He talks about sighs "upon a midnight pillow," and he refuses to believe that anyone could ever have felt the same passion he does. Even so, Rosalind is moved by his declarations of love. She is reminded of her own romantic misfortune—the circumstances of her banishment have kept her away from Orlando. Touchstone responds to Silvius in a different manner entirely. His fanciful account of his courtship of Jane Smile satirizes Silvius' lamentations about the ridiculous actions his love for Phebe have caused him to commit. He was once so much in love, he comments, that he kissed the cows' udders the hands of his beloved had milked. His tale of giving his love two pea pods with the instruction, "wear these for my sake," also parodies Rosalind's gift of a chain to Orlando in the wrestling scene and her request to "Wear this for me."

When Touchstone remarks, "When I was at home, I was in a better place," he wryly argues for the superiority of court life to country life. Again, we are reminded that the life in the forest is perhaps not the ideal paradise of pastoral romance. (Note, also, that Corin's master is of "churlish disposition" and is unlikely "to find the way to heaven" by his deeds.) The long journey to the Forest of Arden and removal from the comforts of home have disillusioned Touchstone, but he pragmatically resigns himself to his fate: "travellers must be content." He promptly seeks to content himself by asserting his authority over one whom he considers his inferior. When he hails Corin in an officious manner and tells him he is being addressed by his "betters," we see further evidence of a new social order. Touchstone, formerly the royal fool, will now assume the role of a sophisticated courtier when he is in the company of shepherds.

Act II, Scene V (pages 25–27)

New Character:

Jacques: *a melancholy philosopher who resides with Duke Senior in the Forest of Arden*

Summary

This scene is set in a clearing in the Forest Arden. Amiens, one of Duke Senior's courtiers, sings a ballad that celebrates the pastoral life. When Amiens concludes his song, Jaques asks for more. Amiens protests that the music will make Jaques melancholy, but Jaques retorts, "I can suck melancholy out of a song as a weasel sucks eggs. More, I prithee, more!" Jaques persists, and finally Amiens agrees to sing another verse. Amiens tells Jaques that Duke Senior has been looking for him, but Jaques replies that he has been deliberately avoiding the Duke. Amiens sings another stanza, and this time his fellow courtiers join in. In the forest, the song concludes, one will find "no enemy/ But winter and rough weather." Jaques promptly invents a verse of his own that satirizes the idealism of Amiens' lyrics: "If it do come to pass/ That any man turn ass,/ Leaving his wealth and ease/ A stubborn will to please . . . Here shall he see gross fools as he." Jaques tells Amiens that he is leaving "to go to sleep, if I can." Amiens tells him that he will go to seek the Duke, whose banquet has been prepared.

Analysis

The song that begins this scene is the first of five songs in the play. Its lyrics, with their images of nature, idealize the pastoral life. Again, we are greeted by a reference to the hazards of "winter and rough weather." Yet the declaration, that it is the only "enemy" one might find in the forest, is another reminder that we are a long way from the envious court.

In this scene, we meet Jaques for the first time. He is a multifaceted character. In Shakespeare's time, he was what was known as a "humors" character. It was common belief at the time that a person's temperament was governed by four "humors," or bodily fluids: blood, yellow bile, black bile, and phlegm. An overabundance of black bile produced melancholy—note that this character is referred to at times as "the melancholy Jaques." Yet melancholy is only one of his moods. In the previous scene, we learned that Jaques had become sentimental and philosophical after discovering the wounded deer. Now we see a more cynical side to his nature.

Like Touchstone, Jaques sees the disadvantages of the pastoral life. Earlier, Touchstone has commented, "now am I in Arden, the more fool, I." In this scene, we hear Jaques saying much the same thing. A man is an ass, he comments, to leave his "wealth and ease" to please his stubborn will in the forest. By nature, he is an argumentative malcontent, eager to take the opposing view to whatever sentiments are expressed by those around him. His satirical parody of Amiens' song typifies his cynicism and contrasts sharply with the idealism of Duke Senior and his court-in-exile.

Act II, Scenes VI and VII (pages 27–33)

Summary

In another part of the forest, we encounter Adam and Orlando. Adam tells Orlando that he is famished, can journey no further, and is ready to die. Orlando comforts him and promises to bring him to shelter; he will then venture forth in search of food.

In Scene VII, Duke Senior, preparing for his banquet, inquires as to Jaques' whereabouts. Jaques enters immediately afterward.

He is in an ebullient mood, having met Touchstone: "A fool, a fool! I met a fool i' the forest." Touchstone, Jaques recounts, had "railed on Lady Fortune in good terms." When Jaques greeted him with "Good morrow, fool," Touchstone replied wittily, "Call me not fool till heaven hath sent me fortune." Touchstone then drew a sundial from his pocket and used it to illustrate his philosophy. At ten o'clock, it is an hour after nine and an hour before eleven; thus, "from hour to hour, we ripe and ripe/ And then from hour to hour, we rot and rot;/ And thereby hangs a tale."

Jaques claims he was so delighted by Touchstone's comments that he laughed an hour by his dial. He expresses the desire that he, too, might be a fool: "I must have liberty . . . give me leave/ To speak my mind, and I will through and through/ Cleanse the foul body of the infected world." Duke Senior remarks that Jaques is an odd choice to do such good, since he has been a libertine. Jaques defends himself by responding that his castigation will not be harmful if he does not name anyone in particular; those who have been criticized justly will realize the truth of his words.

Their exchange comes to a sudden halt when Orlando bursts in with his sword drawn. He commands the Duke and his court to "Forbear, and eat no more!" Jaques replies drolly, "Why, I have eat none yet." Orlando tells him he will not eat until "necessity be served." Duke Senior calmly asks if Orlando has been boldened by his distress and chastises him for his rude manners. Orlando admits that he has been discourteous and tells Duke Senior he has been brought up in civilized society, but he is desperate for food. Duke Senior tells him that force is unnecessary; a gentle request will bring the result he desires. Orlando is surprised by his courtesy: "Speak you so gently? Pardon me, I pray you. I thought that all things had been savage here;/ And therefore put I on the countenance/ Of stern commandment." He apologizes for his behavior, sheathes his sword, and tells Duke Senior that before he can accept any food he must find Adam and bring him to safety. Duke Senior promises that the banquet will not begin until he returns.

After Orlando leaves, Duke Senior, moved by Orlando's suffering, tells his courtiers that "we are not all alone unhappy:/ This wide and universal theatre/ Presents more woeful pageants than the scene/ Wherein we play in." Jaques immediately seizes upon his analogy, commenting: "All the world's a stage,/ And all the men and women merely players;/ They have their exits and their entrances,/ And one man in his time plays many parts,/ His acts being seven ages." He describes each of these ages in turn: the infant, the "whining school-boy," the lover, the soldier, the justice, the "lean and slipper'd/ pantaloon," and finally, "second childishness and mere oblivion."

Orlando enters, carrying Adam in his arms, and the Duke invites them to sit down and eat. Duke Senior asks Amiens to provide some music and Amiens obliges, singing another paean to the pastoral life. After he has finished, Duke Senior tells Orlando that as the son of his old friend, Sir Rowland de Boys, he is welcome to remain. He invites Orlando to come to his cave, welcomes Adam, and asks to hear the story of Orlando's fortunes.

Analysis

Adam's near-starvation in Scene VI further emphasizes the perils of the pastoral life. Like Rosalind, Celia, and Touchstone, Orlando and Adam have had a long and difficult journey. Orlando's devotion to the aged servant again reveals his nobility of character; he repays Adam's kindness with genuine concern.

When we first heard of Jaques he was in a state of despair over the wounded deer; when we saw him first he was sardonic and cynical. At the beginning of Scene VII, we are exposed to another facet of his nature: he is elated, having met Touchstone in the forest. Jaques was ecstatic when Touchstone "railed on Lady Fortune," but he failed to realize that Touchstone was simply parodying his argumentative nature. Touchstone's absurd satire serves to counterbalance Jaques' acerbic criticism of the pastoral life and his cynical view of human nature in general.

This scene features a number of references to time, a motif

that will recur in many variations throughout the play. Touchstone's sundial seems particularly inappropriate in the forest, where little light would reach through the trees. His comment that "from hour to hour we ripe and ripe, / And then, from hour to hour, we rot and rot" is a comic foreshadowing of Jaques' "Seven Ages of Man" speech at the end of this scene. Jaques' assertion that he laughed for an hour by Touchstone's dial is ironic, for again he did not realize that Touchstone was satirizing his philosophy.

Jaques' claim that he longs to be a fool, and thus have liberty to speak his mind freely is also ironic, for he speaks his mind at every opportunity. His declaration that if he, too, could wear motley he could "cleanse the foul body of the infected world" arouses Duke Senior's ire. As one who has sinned, the Duke remarks, he seems an incongruous choice to cure the ills of society. Again, Jaques' observations have some validity, for society, as we have seen it at court, is in need of a cure.

When Duke Senior disarms Orlando with courtesy after Orlando has confronted the Duke and his men with his sword drawn, it is again a reminder than we are in the presence of a new social order, one that is far removed from the "envious court." Orlando's claim to have been well bred seemingly contradicts his statement in Act I, Scene I that he has been denied the education of a gentleman. But we know that he is the son of a father who was much admired, and that he has been gifted by nature with many of Sir Rowland's virtues. His innate good qualities have enabled him to transcend his lack of formal education.

Duke Senior's comment after Orlando leaves to bring Adam to safety that "we are not all alone unhappy" introduces yet another hint that the pastoral life is perhaps not as ideal as many of the characters would have it seem. In Act II, Scene I, Duke Senior extolled his life in the forest, a viewpoint that was echoed in Amiens' first song. Yet here, perhaps because the Duke was reminded of "better days" at court and his own personal misfortune by Orlando's tale of suffering, he admits candidly that there is something "woeful" in his life in exile.

Jaques' "Seven Ages of Man" speech is one of the most famed speeches in all of Shakespeare; it contains some of the Bard's greatest poetry. In this speech, Jaques provides seven impressions of man at varying stages of his life, a further exploration of the theme of time. Yet the canvas he illustrates is selective. For example, we see the infant "mewling and puking" rather than burbling with delight; the schoolboy is "creeping like snail/unwilling to school" rather than making the journey with enthusiasm. Jaques' comments on the lover are in tune with what we have seen of Silvius (and what we will see of Orlando in the scene that follows), but his next two "ages" are limited, for not all men will be soldiers and justices. This speech, in general, reflects the cynical attitude of its speaker rather than offering a well rounded portrait of humanity. Finally, Jaques arrives at old age and the inevitable end: infirmity and death. His tone is rueful and he paints a grim portrait of man "sans teeth, sans eyes, sans taste, sans everything."

By way of contrast, Adam enters immediately afterward. He is almost eighty and weakened by hunger, necessitating that Orlando carry him in his arms. Yet as we know, he is not approaching senility, or "second childishness," as Jaques puts it. He is still vital in spirit, a sharp contrast to Jaques' bleak view of life's fading years.

Jaques' observation that "one man in his time plays many parts" is appropriate, however, for it underscores another major theme of the play: role playing. Rosalind, for example, has been the royal princess and the faithful friend; she has recently assumed the masculine role of Ganymede. Touchstone, as we have seen, played the subservient role of the fool while at court, yet once he is in the Forest of Arden he asserts his superiority to the rustic shepherds, playing the urbane courtier at every opportunity.

Amiens' ballad, "Blow, blow, thou winter wind" is a companion piece to his earlier song. Again, we see a wintery motif juxtaposed with images of a rich, springlike world. This song also echoes the Duke's declaration in Act II, Scene I that "Here feel we not.. the icy fang/ and churlish chiding of the winter's wind." Exposure to the elements, while harsh, is preferable to "man's ingratitude" and "friends rememb'red not." Yet here, a wistful note of skepticism creeps in as well: "Most friendship is feigning, most loving mere folly."

This skepticism is immediately refuted by Duke Senior in

As You Like It

his welcome to Orlando, for he proclaims: "I am the Duke/That loved your father." And as we will see, love, although making many of the characters appear foolish at times, can also have its lasting rewards.

Study Questions

1. Which two characters express sorrow about the killing of deer in the Forest of Arden?

2. Who is the source of the rumor that Orlando may be in the company of Rosalind, Celia, and Touchstone?

3. Why does Adam urge Orlando to avoid his brother's house?

4. Why does Orlando initially refuse to leave?

5. Which three items of property does Rosalind agree to purchase from Corin's employer?

6. What reason does Jaques give for avoiding Duke Senior?

7. Why does Orlando leave Adam in the forest?

8. Which character from the court does Jaques tell Duke Senior he met in the forest?

9. What reasons does Orlando give for confronting Duke Senior and his courtiers with his sword drawn?

10. How does Duke Senior know that Orlando is the son of his former friend and ally, the late Sir Rowland de Boys?

Answers

1. Duke Senior remarks that "it irks me that the poor dappled fools . . . Should in their own confines . . . have their round haunches gored." We also learn that "the melancholy Jaques grieves at that."

2. Hisperia, Celia's waiting gentlewoman, reported that she believed Orlando had accompanied Rosalind, Celia, and Touchstone when they left the court.

3. Adam urges Orlando to leave Oliver's house because Oliver plans to burn Orlando's lodgings while he is asleep. He

also tells Orlando that if this plan fails, Oliver will resort to other treacherous means to kill his brother.

4. Orlando initially refuses to leave because he believes he will be reduced to begging, or that he will be forced to become a thief.

5. Rosalind agrees to purchase a cottage, a flock of sheep, and the pasture land where the sheep graze.

6. Jaques tells Amiens that he is avoiding Duke Senior because "He is too disreputable for my company."

7. Orlando leaves Adam in the forest because he is too weak with hunger to accompany Orlando while he searches for food.

8. Jaques tells Duke Senior that he met Touchstone in the forest.

9. Orlando remarks that he is famished, and he tells Duke Senior, "I thought that all things had been savage here,/ And therefore put I on the countenance/ Of stern commandment."

10. Duke Senior knows that Orlando is the son of the late Sir Rowland de Boys because Orlando has "whispered faithfully" that he was. Duke Senior has also noticed that Orlando's face bears a strong resemblance to his father's.

Suggested Essay Topics

1. Discuss the ways in which Shakespeare reveals that life in the Forest of Arden, while in many ways an idealized existence, also has its hardships.

2. Explore the many images of the natural world in the second act.

3. Compare and contrast the many sides of Jaques' character revealed in the scenes in which he is referred to or appears.

4. Discuss the concept of loyalty as it applies to Orlando and Adam in the second act, and the ways in which it defines their characters.

Act III

Act III, Scenes I and II (pages 34–45)

Summary

At the palace, Duke Frederick commands Oliver to find Orlando and bring him in, dead or alive, within a year. If Oliver fails to do so, his property and goods will be forfeited. Oliver tells Duke Frederick, "I never loved my brother in my life." "More villain thou," Duke Frederick replies. He orders his men to forcibly remove Oliver from the palace and commands that a writ of seizure be placed on Oliver's house and lands.

In Scene II, we return to the Forest of Arden. Orlando, obsessed by his love for Rosalind, writes poems to her and hangs them on trees. After he resolves to carve the name of his beloved on every tree in the forest, he exits.

Corin and Touchstone enter, and Corin asks Touchstone how he likes the shepherd's life. Touchstone replies with a witty series of contradictions. Although he finds some elements of country life appealing, he misses the liveliness of the court and its good manners. Corin tells him bluntly that courtly manners would be out of place in the country. The formal kissing of hands, he comments, would be inappropriate when the hands of shepherds are greasy from handling their sheep. Corin praises the virtues of his simple life as a shepherd, and Touchstone responds with a series of bawdy jests that satirize the shepherd's calling.

Their conversation is interrupted when Rosalind enters in her Ganymede disguise, reading aloud a love poem she has found on a tree: "From the east to western Ind/ No jewel is like Rosalind." Touchstone, unimpressed by the "false gallop" of the verses, promptly invents a parody of the poem. He concludes with yet another bawdy jest. Celia happens upon the scene, reading aloud another love poem about Rosalind.

Celia sends Touchstone and Corin away, and she and Rosalind discuss the poems. Rosalind is critical of their style and literary merit, and she is at a loss to identify their author. When Celia finally tells her, after teasing her for her dullness, that the author can only be Orlando, Rosalind is incredulous. She is ecstatic to learn that Orlando has arrived in the forest, but she wonders how her masculine disguise might complicate matters. "Alas the day!" she remarks. "What shall I do with my doublet and hose?" She queries Celia for any bit of news about Orlando.

Their discussion is interrupted by the entrance of Orlando and Jaques. Rosalind and Celia stand aside and eavesdrop on their conversation. Jaques has taken a cynical view of Orlando's romantic infatuation and urges him to "mar no more trees" with his poems, telling him: "The worst fault you have is to be in love." Orlando proclaims that "'Tis a fault I will not change for your best virtue." Jaques retorts by telling Orlando, "I was looking for a fool when I found you." Orlando chides him by commenting that if it is a fool he is seeking, he can look in the brook, for there he will see his own reflection. They exchange parting shots, and Jaques exits.

Rosalind, in an aside to Celia, resolves to speak to Orlando "like a saucy lackey and under that habit play the knave with him." She steps forward and addresses the young man, who does not recognize her in her Ganymede disguise. They banter lightheartedly about time and love. Rosalind cautions Orlando that love is a disease that is best cured. She tells him that "There is a man haunts the forest that abuses our young plants with carving 'Rosalind' on their barks, hangs odes on hawthorns, and elegies on brambles . . . If I could meet that fancy-monger, I would give him some good counsel." Orlando confesses that "I am he that is so love-shaked" and asks for her remedy. Rosalind wittily catalogues the physical symptoms of a man in love, and she remarks that Orlando seems to have none of them. Orlando protests that he is indeed in love, but Rosalind tells him that "love is merely a madness" and proposes "curing it." She tells him she has, in the past, cured a lovelorn swain of his "mad humor" by impersonating his fickle mistress, "full of tears" one minute, "full of smiles" the next. She promises that she can heal Orlando's love-sickness as well. Orlando declares that he does not want to be cured, but Ganymede tells him a cure is possible if Orlando will call "him" Rosalind and come to "his" cottage every day to court him. Orlando, pleased by the thought of wooing even a surrogate Rosalind, agrees to the plan.

Analysis

Scene I brings the two villains of the play together. Oliver, accustomed to issuing commands to Orlando, now must answer to a more powerful tyrant. Ironically, Duke Frederick remarks that Oliver is a villain for failing to love his brother. Frederick is guilty of this same offense. This brief scene also sets the stage for Oliver's arrival in the Forest of Arden.

In Scene II, we see Orlando behaving just as Jaques commented the lover does in his "Seven Ages of Man" speech: "Sighing like furnace, with a woeful ballad/Made to his mistress's eyebrow." Here, he is the lovestruck poet of Renaissance tradition. His verses leave something to be desired, but their sentiments are evidently sincere.

Later in this scene, Corin, in his exchange with Touchstone, eloquently defends the virtues of the pastoral life: "I earn that I eat, get that I wear, owe no man hate, envy no man's happiness, glad of other men's good, content with my harm, and the greatest of my pride is to see my ewes graze and my lambs suck." Touchstone, playing the role of a dissatisfied exile, argues wittily that the court, with its good manners, is far superior to the countryside. His speech features a host of amusing contradictions, and at the same time it satirizes the pastoral ideal. But Corin, praising the reality of his rural existence rather than the ideal notions of the pastoral life expressed by Duke Senior and others, rebuts him on nearly all of the points he makes. Here, we are greeted once more by the theme of city life versus country life. Note that Corin, unlike Silvius, is not an idealized shepherd, but rather a more realistically drawn figure who is concerned primarily with the practical details of his trade.

Touchstone's parody of Orlando's poem is apt, for the poem Rosalind has read has a syrupy, sentimental quality and a number of awkward rhymes. Touchstone's bawdy jest at the end of his parody echoes his bawdy comments to Corin in their earlier exchange. His references to sexuality and lust, here and elsewhere, satirize the idealized notions of love expressed by many of the other characters.

The Orlando-Jaques dialogue parallels in its contrasts the Corin-Touchstone exchange in this scene. Earlier we had seen a pairing of opposites in the sophisticated wit and the simple shepherd. Here we see the worldly cynic and the romantic innocent engage in a duel of words. Jaques would like nothing better than to sit down with Orlando and "rail against our mistress the world, and all our misery." Yet Orlando, true to his nature, will have none of it. The attitudes toward romance expressed by Orlando and Jaques reflect the timeless conflicts of youth and age. Orlando's refutation of Jaques' skepticism serves as a prologue to the love scene that follows. Later, Rosalind's encounter with Jaques will serve much the same purpose.

When Rosalind and Orlando banter about time, it recalls Jaques' mention of Touchstone's sundial in an earlier scene. Again, reference to time seems ironic, for while court life (which Touchstone can never escape entirely) is strictly regimented, the Forest of Arden is in many ways a timeless place. As Orlando remarks, "there's no clock in the forest." This comment foreshadows his behavior in later scenes. Rosalind, on the other hand, is far more conscious of time's passing, a disparity that will lead to complications in her relationship with the man she loves. She tells Orlando bluntly that if there is no clock in the forest, "Then, there is no true lover in the forest; else sighing every minute, and groaning every hour, would detect the lazy foot of Time as well as a clock." In sum, if Orlando were a true lover, he would be prompt.

This scene features a number of incongruities. It seems unlikely, for example, that Rosalind, intelligent and quick-witted, would not know immediately that the author of the mysterious love poems is Orlando. We are also asked to accept the fact that Orlando does not recognize the woman he claims to love in her Ganymede disguise. Much of the humor here arises from confusion—the inability of a character to perceive what other characters already know. The audience (or the reader) is also in on the "secret." This type of confusion occurs frequently in Shakespeare's comedies.

Indeed, the entire Forest of Arden is filled with incongruities. The play is set in the Ardennes region of France (note the French names of many of the characters), but the forest is home to a palm tree and olive trees; later, we will hear that a lioness roams there as well. Moreover, the countryside is peopled by typically English shepherds, and there is a reference to the English folk hero, Robin Hood. In fact, there is a real-life Forest of Arden in Warwickshire, not far from Stratford-upon-Avon where Shakespeare was born and raised. No attempt is made, however, to depict this location realistically. Arden is a place that is both real and enchanted.

Initially, Rosalind is panic-stricken upon learning that Orlando had arrived in the forest; she wonders what to do with her doublet and hose. For the moment, she feels trapped in the role she has assumed. Earlier, she had asked Celia, "dost thou think, though I am caparison'd like a man, I have a doublet and hose in my disposition?" However, when Orlando appears, she quickly recovers her wits and realizes that her disguise may, in fact, prove an advantage. Later, when Orlando becomes suspicious of her refined accent, she invents a "history" for her character, telling Orlando she was raised by "an old religious uncle" who taught her to speak and warned her about the folly of love. She asks Orlando bluntly, "But are you so much in love as your rhymes speak?" Although he has written poetry, she remarks, Orlando seems to have none of the traditional signs of a man in love: a lean cheek, disarray in his dress, and so on. She then sets in motion a plan to put Orlando's love to the test by attempting to "cure" him of his "malady." She refers to Orlando's declarations of love as a "sickness," and she disparages the ways of women. When she impersonated a woman in the past to cure another lovelorn swain, she remarks, her methods were so effective that her "suitor" withdrew to a monastery.

Orlando is initially reluctant to be cured, yet ultimately he agrees to the plan. By the end of this scene, Rosalind is clearly in control and relishes her situation. Her playful yet serious investigation of Orlando's true feelings for her will continue in scenes to come.

Act III, Scenes III–V (pages 46–54)

New Characters:

Audrey: *a country wench*

Sir Oliver Martext: *a clergyman*

Phebe: *a shepherdess who dwells near the Forest of Arden*

Summary

Touchstone, in a merry mood, enters with Audrey, a goatherd who lives near the Forest of Arden. Jaques also arrives on the scene; he stands aside, eavesdropping on their conversation. Touchstone attempts to woo Audrey, asking, "Am I the man yet? Doth my simple feature content you?" His witticisms are lost on the simple country goatherd, who does not understand the meaning of the word "poetical." Touchstone has no illusions about Audrey's morals; he suspects her of being a "foul slut." Audrey protests that she is not "a slut," but she adds, "I thank the gods I am foul." Jaques, in a series of asides, comments cynically on the scene that is unfolding.

Touchstone tells Audrey that he has met with Sir Oliver Martext, a clergyman who lives nearby. Sir Oliver has promised to meet him in the forest to perform a marriage ceremony. Touchstone realizes, however, that after he is married to Audrey she is likely to be unfaithful to him. He wittily resigns himself to this fact.

Sir Oliver Martext arrives and Touchstone asks him to officiate at the wedding, but Sir Oliver comments that the marriage will not be lawful unless someone is there to give the bride away. Jaques immediately steps forward to volunteer his services. He comments that a man of Touchstone's "breeding" should not be "married under a bush like a beggar" and urges him to go to a

As You Like It

church, where a "good priest" might marry him. Touchstone, in an aside, remarks that he prefers to be married by Sir Oliver, for the marriage might not be legal, thus leaving him free to abandon his wife and make a better marriage. He agrees to listen to Jaques' advice, however, and proclaims, "Come, sweet Audrey. / We must be married, or we must live in bawdry." He exits with Jaques and Audrey, singing merrily, while a bewildered Sir Oliver stares after them.

In Scene IV, Rosalind, close to tears, worries that Orlando may have forsaken her because he has not arrived at the scheduled time for their meeting. Celia reminds her that tears are inappropriate to her masculine disguise; she reassures her cousin that Orlando is simply attending Duke Senior. Rosalind tells Celia that she had met the Duke the previous day. Her father had not recognized her in her disguise, and when the Duke inquired of her parentage, Rosalind answered wittily that it was "as good as he."

Corin enters and tells Rosalind and Celia that Silvius, the lovelorn shepherd they had often asked about, is at that moment wooing Phebe, the shepherdess he loves. Corin remarks that if they would care to "see a pageant truly play'd/Between the pale complexion of true love/ And the red glow of scorn and proud disdain" they are welcome to accompany him. Rosalind agrees, commenting: "The sight of lovers feedeth those in love./ Bring us to this sight, and you shall say/ I'll prove a busy actor in their play."

Scene V takes place in a nearby part of the forest. Silvius begs the disdainful Phebe for even the smallest kindness: "Sweet Phebe, do not scorn me; do not, Phebe;/ Say that you love me not, but say not so/ In bitterness." Rosalind, Celia, and Corin enter and observe their conversation from a distance. Silvius tells Phebe that if she falls in love one day she will sympathize with his anguish. However Phebe tells him bluntly, "till that time/ Come not thou near me. . . . As till that time I shall not pity thee."

At this point, Rosalind steps forward to interrupt their conversation. She angrily chastises Phebe for being "proud and pitiless," and she tells Silvius that he is foolish to pursue Phebe, since Silvius is "a thousand times a properer man/ Than she is a woman." Phebe, Rosalind remarks, should be thankful to have a good man's love, since she is not the charming beauty she thinks herself to be. "Sell when you can," Rosalind admonishes her, "you are not for all markets." She urges Phebe to love Silvius and to "take his offer" of marriage.

By that time, however, Phebe has become hopelessly captivated by Rosalind in her Ganymede disguise. Rosalind attempts to discourage her interest by speaking harshly, telling her, "I am falser than vows made in wine" and "I like you not." She urges Silvius to keep at his courtship, and she tells Phebe to "look on him better/And be not proud." With that, she turns and exits with Celia and Corin.

Phebe instantly confesses that now she understands what it means to love. Transformed by her encounter with Ganymede, she admits that she feels sorry for Silvius. Again, she tells the lovelorn shepherd that she has no romantic interest in him, but since he can talk of love, she will tolerate his company. She contradicts her statement of a moment earlier, however, by claiming petulantly that Ganymede, though attractive in certain ways, does not really interest her. She resolves to write a taunting letter to the "peevish boy" to repay him for his rudeness. Silvius agrees to deliver the letter after it is written.

Analysis

Touchstone's courting of Audrey in Scene III represents a different type of love than those we have already seen. He candidly confesses to Jaques his reasons for wanting to marry his earthy goatherd: "as the ox hath his bow, sir, the horse his curb, and the falcon her bells, so man hath his desires." Here, he burlesques the romantic idealism we have seen in Orlando and Silvius. He is not seeking beauty and wit; he merely wishes to fulfill his physical cravings.

Touchstone's obscene jests with Audrey were a convention of Elizabethan comedy, one that Shakespeare's audience would have looked forward to eagerly. When Touchstone engages in a witty yet introspective series of puns comparing a deer's antlers to the "horns" he expects to wear, he is creating a variation on one of the most popular jokes in Shakespeare's time. In Elizabethan England, "horns" were the symbol of a cuckold, a man whose wife was cheating on him. The world "cuckold" is derived from the cuckoo—a bird that lays its eggs in other birds' nests. According to Elizabethan legend, cuckolds grew horns on their foreheads. Touchstone, pragmatic about the future, resigns himself to the fact that this will be his inevitable fate if he marries Audrey.

Scene IV reveals Rosalind's insecurities about Orlando's true feelings for her. She also discloses the extent of her love for Orlando. She is upset with him for not arriving at the scheduled time of their meeting, but Celia, a calm voice of reason, assures her that Orlando is busy attending Duke Senior. Again, we are greeted by the theme of role playing when Corin invites Rosalind and Celia to witness "a pageant truly played" by observing Silvius' courtship of Phebe, and in Rosalind's subsequent declaration that she will "prove a busy actor in their play."

Lovelorn shepherds such as Silvius were a convention of pastoral romance. In Scene V, Shakespeare satirizes those conventions by depicting Silvius' unrequited passion as comically excessive. There seems to be no end to his misery. Here, we are exposed to yet another aspect of love. Silvius is much like Orlando in his ardor, but instead of writing poems, he sighs pathetically about the "wounds invisible/ That love's keen arrows make." It is easy to see why Phebe might be weary of his relentless pursuit. Yet Phebe, as Rosalind points out, is no prize herself. She is vain, petulant, and hindered by her false pride. Just as Shakespeare satirizes the lovelorn shepherd in Silvius, he satirizes another familiar literary type, the "poetic shepherdess," in Phebe. Note that Audrey, a rustic goatherd, did not understand the meaning of the word "poetical," yet Phebe speaks in verse and quotes from a poem by one of Shakespeare's contemporaries, Christopher Marlowe, when she proclaims, "Who ever loved that loved not at first sight?"

Rosalind's harsh criticism of the shepherdess has the opposite effect of what is intended, for Phebe is immediately captivated by Rosalind in her Ganymede disguise. Nevertheless, she craftily misleads Silvius by disparaging Ganymede and playing down the extent of her interest. Thus, additional comic complications are added to the plot as the third act draws to a close.

Study Questions

1. What penalty will Oliver face if he fails to find Orlando within a year?

2. What does Orlando do with the love poems he has written to Rosalind?

3. Where does Celia tell Rosalind she saw Orlando?

4. Where does Orlando tell Jaques he can find a fool?

5. What names do Jaques and Orlando call each other when they part?

6. What excuse does Rosalind make when Orlando comments that her accent seems "something finer" than one might expect of a native of the forest?

7. Why does Touchstone prefer to be married by Sir Oliver Martext rather than "a good priest?"

8. What did Ganymede tell Duke Senior when the Duke asked about her parentage?

9. How do we know that Phebe has fallen in love with Rosalind in her Ganymede disguise?

10. What message does Phebe plan to deliver to Ganymede and who will deliver it?

Answers

1. Duke Frederick tells Oliver that if he fails to find Orlando within a year, he will forfeit his lands and goods.

2. Orlando hangs the love poems he has written to Rosalind on trees in the Forest of Arden.

3. Celia tells Rosalind that she saw Orlando "under a tree, like a dropped acorn."

4. Orlando tells Jaques to look in the brook if he is seeking a fool, for there he will see his own reflection.

5. Jaques calls Orlando "Signior Love." Orlando calls Jaques "Monsieur Melancholy."

6. Rosalind tells Orlando that "an old religious uncle" of hers, in his youth a city man, had taught her how to speak.

7. Touchstone prefers to be married by Sir Oliver Martext because he believes that the marriage might not be legal, thus leaving him free to eventually abandon his wife.

8. When Duke Senior, not recognizing his daughter in her disguise, inquired of Rosalind's parentage, she told him her parentage was "as good as he."

9. We know that Phebe has fallen in love with Ganymede when she comments after Rosalind's exit, "'Who ever loved that loved not at first sight?'"

10. Phebe plans to write a "taunting letter" to Ganymede for scorning her. She asks Silvius to deliver the letter, and he agrees.

Suggested Essay Topics

1. Compare and contrast the attitudes toward love expressed by Orlando, Touchstone, Jaques, and Silvius in the third act.

2. Compare and contrast the attitudes of Corin and Touchstone toward country life and city life in Act III, Scene II.

3. Explore the ways that Rosalind's Ganymede disguise affects her behavior in this act.

4. Discuss the ways in which the developments in the third act foreshadow further comic complications.

SECTION FIVE

Act IV

Act IV, Scene I (pages 55–60)

Summary

Rosalind and Celia, still in their disguises, enter with Jaques, who expresses a desire to become better acquainted with Ganymede. Rosalind comments that she has heard that Jaques is "a melancholy fellow." Jaques admits this is true; he tells Rosalind that he likes melancholy better than laughter. Rosalind cautions against going to extremes of either melancholy or mirth, and Jaques retorts that " 'tis good to be sad and say nothing." In that case, Rosalind replies wittily, it is good to be a post. Jaques remarks that his melancholy was acquired during his travels abroad, but Rosalind is skeptical of his tale. Orlando enters soon afterward. Jaques bids farewell to Ganymede and departs.

Orlando, late for his rendezvous, casually explains to Rosalind that he has come within an hour of the appointed time. Rosalind chides him for being tardy; true lovers, she reminds him, arrive promptly. She tells him, "I had as lief be wooed of a snail," and she adds mischievously that a snail, like many husbands, has "horns." Women, she reminds him, can't be trusted to be faithful. Orlando protests that his Rosalind is virtuous. "And I am your Rosalind," Ganymede proclaims, elated by the compliment. Celia, worried that Orlando might realize the truth of this statement, quickly interjects, "It pleaseth him to call you so: but he hath a Rosalind of a better leer than you." However Orlando is none the wiser, and Ganymede bids Orlando to "Come, woo me." She asks Orlando what he would say if the "real" Rosalind were there. Orlando replies that he would kiss before he spoke. Rosalind tells him bluntly it would be better to speak first. After bantering merrily with Orlando, Ganymede plays the devil's advocate, telling him, "I will not have you."

Orlando protests that he would die if this were the case, but Rosalind replies skeptically that "men have died from time to time and worms have eaten them, but not for love." Orlando tells her he would not have his Rosalind "of this mind," for her frown might kill him. Ganymede then agrees to play Rosalind in a more receptive mood. "Ask me what you will, I will grant it," she remarks. Orlando asks her to love him. Rosalind, as Ganymede, replies that she will, "Fridays and Saturdays and all," although she jests that she will also have twenty more men like him, since one cannot have "too much of a good thing." She then asks Celia to perform a mock marriage ceremony. Rosalind and Orlando exchange vows with Celia serving as "priest," but when they have finished, Ganymede cautions that women often change after they are married. She warns Orlando that his Rosalind will be jealous, clamorous, and giddy, will "weep for nothing," and will "laugh like a hyena" when he is trying to sleep.

Orlando tells Ganymede that he must leave for two hours to attend Duke Senior at dinner, but he promises to return. Rosalind warns him not to be late again, telling him that another lateness will prove him a "most pathetical break-promise" and a man unworthy of Rosalind's love. With a pledge to return on time, Orlando exits.

After he is gone, Celia chides Rosalind for having "misused our sex" in her role playing with Orlando. She jokingly threatens to pull off her doublet and hose to reveal her masquerade. Rosalind protests that she is more deeply in love than Celia realizes; My affection hath an unknown bottom, like the Bay of Portugal." She tells Celia that she cannot bear to be out of Orlando's sight and plans to "go find a shadow, and sigh till he come." While Rosalind is sighing, Celia will be doing something far more mundane: taking a nap.

Analysis

Rosalind's reaction to Jaques is similar to Orlando's response in an earlier scene. Again, we are greeted by a classic conflict between youth and age. Rosalind would rather have a fool to make her merry than experience to make her sad. Her romanticism, like Orlando's, stands in sharp contrast to Jaques' cynical view of the world.

In this scene, Jaques attempts to define his melancholy as unique, commenting that it is unlike the scholar's melancholy, the musician's, the soldier's, the lawyer's, the lover's, or the lady's. In sum, he briefly catalogues the varieties of melancholy as he had previously categorized the ages of man at greater length. Elizabethan audiences took particular delight in complex flights of rhetoric such as Jaques offers here; earlier, we heard similarly detailed discussions of fortune, nature, and time.

Jaques remarks that his world weariness is a result of his travels abroad. To Rosalind, however, his speech, dress, and general demeanor seem merely an exaggerated pose. Here, Shakespeare was satirizing the Englishmen of his own time who returned from the Continent and expressed dissatisfaction with life at home. Earlier, Touchstone had stated that "Travellers must be content." Jaques, on the other hand, asserts that his travels have made him a malcontent. We already know that Duke Senior likes to contend with Jaques when he is in his melancholy moods, but he does not take him seriously. Rosalind, the Duke's daughter, seems even less impressed by Jaques' gloomy philosophy.

When Orlando enters the scene, he is almost an hour late for his appointment with Ganymede. Apparently he is caught up in the timelessness of the forest, but Rosalind is not. Jaques notices him when he enters, but Rosalind, peeved at his lateness, ignores him. She comments on the departing Jaques for a moment before turning to greet him with mock surprise: "Why, how now, Orlando, where have you been all this while?" One more lateness, she warns him, and he will be banished from her sight.

Clearly, Rosalind is delighted by the opportunity to again "play the saucy lackey" with the man she loves. The character of Rosalind is one of Shakespeare's most vivacious, charismatic heroines. She is witty and wise, with a playful sense of humor, yet she, too, is not immune to the wonders of love. When she proclaims to Orlando, "I am your Rosalind," she is, of course, speaking the truth. Celia is concerned that Orlando might see through Rosalind's disguise, but Orlando, in keeping with the play's conventions, gives no indication that he suspects Ganymede's true identity.

As Ganymede, Rosalind has the opportunity to present Orlando with not one but two Rosalinds. The first is somewhat of a skeptic. Playfully, she puts Orlando to the test, mocking his romantic assertions that he will die if Rosalind rejects him. (Note that Orlando, in his comments, echoes Silvius' remarks to Phebe in the previous scene that he, too, will die if Phebe does not love him.) Rosalind quickly rebuts his conventional sentiments, citing the supposedly tragic examples from classical literature of Troilus and Cressida and Hero and Leander. She tells him bluntly, "These are all lies." However when Orlando objects to Ganymede's "characterization," Rosalind tries a different approach: playing "Rosalind" in a more pliant mood. She enjoys hearing Orlando's declarations of love, and her own responses to his wooing and genuine, both here and in the mock wedding that follows.

Afterward, however, she cautions Orlando that "Men are like April when they woo, December when they wed. Maids are May when they are maids, but the sky changes when they are wives." Given the many contrasts we have already seen between the green world of spring and the "icy fang" of winter, her analogy seems apt. Yet here again, Rosalind is playing devil's advocate. She is putting Orlando to the test with generalized observations on the foibles of human nature rather than predicting what might occur in her own marriage. Her comments on "horns" and infidelity, for instance, are made playfully rather than in earnest.

There is probably some truth in Ganymede's warning to Orlando about the "irrational" behavior he might expect from his wife, however, given what we have already seen of Rosalind's many moods. Yet Orlando is undaunted, and Rosalind is reluctant to see him depart to attend the Duke. His response to Ganymede has made it obvious that he loves the "real" Rosalind. After he is gone, Rosalind abandons her role playing. She confesses to Celia that she is deeply in love. However Celia wryly punctures Rosalind's romanticism with bawdy jests and skepticism, just as Rosalind has teased Orlando moments earlier.

Note that Celia, although present throughout this scene, plays a diminishing role as the play progresses. Earlier, Celia commented that the cousins "have slept together,/ Rose at an instant, learned, played, eat together,/ And wheresoe'r we went, like Juno's swans,/ Still we went coupled and inseparable." Yet now we see their relationship changing; Celia is almost silent as Rosalind and Orlando engage in their courting. She is watching her friend's affections being shifted to Orlando, and we are aware that the longstanding relations between the two loving cousins will be transformed as they move toward maturity and marriage.

Act IV, Scene II (page 60)

Summary

In another part of the forest, Jaques encounters several Lords bearing the carcass of a deer. He asks which of the Lords killed the deer and suggests that they "present him to the Duke, like a Roman conquerer." He inquires if they have a song for the occasion, which they do. "Sing it," Jaques commands. "'Tis no matter how it be in tune, so it make noise enough." The Lords break into a lusty song that features a play on words comparing a deer's antlers and the "horns" of a cuckold.

Analysis

Jaques' response to meeting the Lords and seeing their slaughtered prey is in sharp contrast to his "weeping and commenting" after encountering a wounded deer in the second act. His response suggests that there may be some truth to Rosalind's accusation that his melancholy and cynicism may in part be a pose. However, there is more than a hint of sarcasm in his suggestion that the deer be given to the Duke like tribute paid to a Roman conquerer.

The lyrics to the song, with their references to "horns" and cuckoldry, again evoke a comic motif we have heard in the conversations of Touchstone and Rosalind. Touchstone's comments have been witty yet pragmatic, given that he is planning to marry Audrey, and Rosalind's remarks were designed principally to put Orlando to the test by disparaging women's virtues and romantic love in general. Here, the song seems designed to counterbalance the lyrical romanticism of Rosalind's declarations at the end of the previous scene. Note that Shakespeare often juxtaposes romantic sentiments with a refutation of the romantic ideal. After Rosalind reads aloud one of Orlando's poems, for example, we are greeted by Touchstone's bawdy parody.

Act IV, Scene III (pages 61–66)

Summary

It is now past two o'clock, the appointed hour of Rosalind and Orlando's meeting, but Orlando has not appeared. Celia teases Rosalind by telling her that Orlando is so deeply in love that he has probably fallen asleep.

Silvius enters and presents Ganymede with the letter Phebe has written to her. He confesses that he does not know the contents, but tells her that he believes the letter was written in anger, judging by Phebe's expression while she was writing it. Rosalind pretends to Silvius that Phebe has been harsh in her criticism of Ganymede. She playfully accuses Silvius of writing the letter himself and comments that it appears to be in a man's handwriting. But Silvius innocently denies any knowledge of the letter's contents.

Rosalind reads the letter aloud, insisting all the while that Phebe is insulting Ganymede. However it is actually a love letter, and when Silvius hears Phebe's impassioned sentiments he realizes the truth and is heartbroken. Celia feels sorry for Silvius, but

Rosalind comments that he is foolish to love a woman as false as Phebe. She commands Silvius to return to the shepherdess to inform her that Ganymede will love her only when she loves Silvius. She also tells him to deliver the message that Ganymede will "never have her" unless Silvius pleads for her cause. Silvius exits meekly to do her bidding.

A stranger enters immediately afterward, inquiring as to the whereabouts of "that youth" whom Orlando "calls his Rosalind." It is Orlando's brother Oliver, and he is bearing a token from Orlando: a bloody handkerchief. He explains why Orlando was unable to keep his promise to return at two o'clock. While wandering in the forest, Orlando had come across "a wretched, ragged man, o'er grown with hair" sleeping beneath an ancient oak tree. A snake was entwined around his neck, but seeing Orlando, the snake slithered away. Greater peril lay nearby, however, for a hungry lioness was lurking in the bushes. Orlando saw the lioness, yet approached the sleeping man and discovered that it was his brother who had plotted to take his life. Twice, Orlando thought about leaving Oliver in peril, but his kind nature, "nobler ever than revenge," led him to wrestle with the lioness, whom he quickly killed.

Oliver admits to Rosalind and Celia that he is the man Orlando rescued, the same man who had often contrived to kill his younger brother. He tells them that he is no longer the villain he once was; grateful to Orlando for saving his life, he has reconciled with his brother. After Oliver related to Orlando the story of how he had arrived in the forest, Orlando had taken him to meet Duke Senior. While visiting the Duke at his cave, Orlando discovered that the lioness had wounded his arm. Oliver bound his wound, and Orlando had sent his brother into the forest with the bloody handkerchief to find "the shepherd youth/ That he in sport doth call his Rosalind," and to apologize for his missed appointment. When Rosalind hears that Orlando has been wounded and realizes the handkerchief is stained with his blood, she faints.

Oliver, unaware that Ganymede is Rosalind in disguise, observes that "many will swoon when they look on blood," but he chides her for lacking "a man's heart." Rosalind acknowledges that his last statement is true, but she makes the excuse that she was simply absorbed in her role. She asks Oliver to tell his brother "how well I counterfeited." Yet Oliver observes that Ganymede's passion for Orlando seems real. Celia remarks that Ganymede looks pale, and Oliver and Celia lead her away toward her cottage.

Analysis

Orlando, as we have seen, is a young man of many virtues, but promptness is not one of them. In the first scene of the act, he was warned by Rosalind that his next lateness would be his last, thus setting up potential complications if he is late to their next meeting. But this time, as we learn, he has a good excuse.

Rosalind, as Ganymede, toys with Silvius in much the same way as she had teased Orlando in Act IV, Scene I. She pretends that Phebe's letter is what Silvius had supposed it to be, and she accuses him of writing it himself. Here again, Phebe is in many ways the "poetic shepherdess" of pastoral romance (her love letter is, of course written in verse), yet Rosalind punctures the convention by making fun of her "leathery" hands. When she realizes how upset Silvius is by the actual contents of the letter, she becomes justifiably irate at his infatuation, calling him a "tame snake." She then institutes a practical plan that may cure Phebe of her false pride and bring the lovers together.

Oliver's conversion seems miraculous. However, such instantaneous changes were a convention of Elizabethan drama, one that Shakespeare's audience would have accepted. The play, as we have seen, contains a number of realistic elements, yet Oliver's transformation is in keeping with the fairy tale nature of much of the story. Even so, his metamorphosis may not have been as sudden as it might seem. Oliver, when last seen in Act III, Scene I was banished by a more powerful tyrant than himself, and we learn that he wandered extensively, enduring the hardships of the forest, perhaps giving him reasons to contemplate his actions in the past.

Throughout much of the play, Rosalind demonstrates "masculine" confidence while in her disguise. Yet she loses her courage when she is confronted by the sight of the handkerchief soaked with Orlando's blood. Much of the comedy in the latter part of this scene results from Rosalind behaving in an "unmasculine" manner. The dialogue features a good deal of dramatic irony: Oliver, for example, chides Ganymede for lacking a man's heart, and Ganymede comments, "I should have been a woman by right." Rosalind has "counterfeited" her outward appearance to play the role of Ganymede (and indeed, she claims to Oliver that she has counterfeited a woman so well that she faints at the sight of blood), yet her emotions are genuine.

Oliver, like his brother, is fooled by Rosalind's disguise, although by the end of this scene it is apparent that the disguise is wearing thin. (Note that Celia slips in calling Rosalind "Cousin Ganymede.") Orlando has now been put to the test and has passed; again, we feel the depth of Rosalind's love for him. The masquerade is rapidly losing its attraction, and the events of the play are winding to a close.

Study Questions

1. What is Rosalind's response when Orlando fears "her frown might kill" him?

2. Who performs the mock wedding ceremony between Rosalind and Orlando?

3. How long does Orlando say he will be gone before he returns to Rosalind?

4. What excuse does Orlando give for leaving?

5. What question does Jaques ask the Lords he meets in the forest?

6. What did Orlando ask Oliver to bring to Ganymede?

7. Which two animals threatened Oliver while he slept beneath a tree?

8. What wound did Orlando receive while defending his brother?

9. What is Rosalind's response when she hears that Orlando has been injured?

10. Where does Rosalind say she would like to be after she recovers?

Answers

1. Rosalind, as Ganymede, tells Orlando that his Rosalind "would not kill a fly."

2. Celia performs the mock wedding ceremony.

3. Orlando says he will be gone for two hours.

4. Orlando tells Rosalind he must leave to "attend the Duke at dinner."

5. Jaques asks the Lords which of them has killed the deer they are bearing to the Duke.

6. Orlando asked Oliver to bring Ganymede a handkerchief soaked with his blood.

7. Oliver was threatened by a "green and gilded snake" and a lioness.

8. Orlando had flesh torn away on his arm while battling the lioness.

9. When Rosalind learns that Orlando has been injured, she faints.

10. When she regains consciousness, Rosalind comments, "I would I were at home."

Suggested Essay Topics

1. Examine the ways that Rosalind tests Orlando's love for her in Act IV, Scene I.

2. Explore the ways in which what we have already learned about Orlando foreshadows his courageous actions in saving his brother's life.

3. Discuss the ways that Rosalind's Ganymede disguise proves an advantage and a disadvantage in Act IV, Scenes I and III.

4. Contrast the changing roles of Celia and Oliver in the fourth act with their characterizations earlier in the play.

SECTION SIX

Act V

Act V, Scene I (pages 67–68)

New Character:

William: *a simpleminded young man*

Summary

    Touchstone asks Audrey to be patient; he assures her that their marriage will indeed take place. Audrey argues that Sir Oliver Martext was good enough to perform the ceremony, but Touchstone disparages the cleric and moves on to another topic, remarking that there is a youth in the forest who "lays claim" to Audrey. However Audrey, interested only in marrying her urbane man of the court, protests that her supposed suitor "hath no interest in me in the world."

    William, an unsophisticated young man of twenty-five, enters. As soon as Touchstone sees his potential rival, he decides to have some fun at his expense. He questions William about his background and inquires as to whether he loves Audrey. William replies that he does. Touchstone officiously asks William if he is "learned." When William replies that he is not, Touchstone launches into an absurd flight of rhetoric that "proves" his right to wed Audrey. The dumbfounded William fails to comprehend.

    Touchstone then asserts his claim to the country goatherd in plainer language. He tells William to abandon his courtship, declaring that if he does not he will kill him a hundred and fifty different ways. "Therefore," he concludes, "tremble and depart."

To this, Audrey adds her own simple pronouncement: "Do, good William." William meekly agrees and exits. Corin enters immediately afterward and tells Touchstone and Audrey that Ganymede and Aliena are seeking them.

Analysis

William is a genuine rustic, the type of character one might have expected to encounter in a rural setting in Shakespeare's time. He stands in sharp contrast to Silvius, a poetic shepherd drawn not from life but from the conventions of pastoral romance. Touchstone deceives the unlearned William, just as he has fooled Audrey, with his displays of "erudition." There is a comic contrast in the polite way that William addresses Touchstone and Touchstone's condescending tone when speaking to his rustic "rival." William uses the polite "you" when speaking to Touchstone, but Touchstone employs a patronizing "thou" in speaking to one whom he considers his inferior. Touchstone's threats, of course, are not to be taken seriously, and his aggressive manner disappears as soon as William exits.

Act V, Scenes II and III (pages 69–73)

Summary

Orlando has learned that Oliver has fallen in love with Aliena at first sight. He is incredulous at the news, but Oliver assures his brother that his love is genuine and asks for his permission to marry. He tells Orlando that after he is married he plans to give him their father's house "and all the revenue that was old Sir Rowland's." Furthermore, Oliver plans to "here live and die a shepherd." Orlando grants his consent. He tells Oliver that the wedding will take place the next day and bids him to invite the Duke and his followers.

Rosalind enters, still disguised as Ganymede. After she exchanges greetings with Oliver he departs. She tells Orlando that she had been distressed to hear of the wounds he suffered in his battle with the lioness, but Orlando is more worried about his romantic affairs. Rosalind remarks upon Oliver and Aliena's love for each other and predicts a happy marriage. Orlando replies that he is sad to "look into happiness through another man's eyes," for his own romantic situation seems far less promising.

Rosalind asks if she couldn't again serve as Orlando's Rosalind on the day of the wedding. But Orlando answers that he can "no longer live by thinking." Rosalind assures him that she has a solution to his problem. Since the age of three, she comments, she has "conversed with a magician" who has taught her the secrets of his art. She promises that when Oliver marries Aliena, Orlando will marry his Rosalind as well. She pledges to produce the real Rosalind the next day. Orlando is skeptical, but Ganymede reaffirms "his" promise and tells Orlando to dress in his best clothes and invite his friends to his own wedding.

Silvius and Phebe enter, and Phebe promptly criticizes Ganymede for showing her letter to Silvius. Rosalind tells her that it was her intention to be "despiteful and ungentle." She remarks that Silvius is a faithful shepherd and tells Phebe to love him, for he worships her. Silvius again declares his love for Phebe, but the shepherdess protests that she is in love with Ganymede. Orlando then proclaims his love for Rosalind. With Phebe's infatuation in mind, Rosalind announces that she is "for no woman." The lovers repeat their declarations until finally Rosalind wearies of their sighing: "Pray you, no more of this; 'tis like the howling of Irish wolves against the moon." She pledges to help Silvius if she can; she tells Phebe that she would love her if she could and requests a meeting the next day, promising, "I will marry you if ever I marry a woman, and I'll be married tomorrow." To Orlando, she remarks that she will satisfy him if ever she satisfied a man; she assures him that he will be married the next day. She also promises Silvius that he will be married at the same time.

In Scene III, Touchstone announces to Audrey that they, too, will be married on the morrow. Two Pages enter, and Touchstone requests a song. The Pages respond by singing "It was a Lover and his Lass," a merry song that celebrates love, marriage, and the pastoral life. When the Pages have finished, Touchstone criticizes the song and their singing: "I count it but time lost to hear such a foolish song. God b' wi' you, and God mend your voices."

Analysis

The notion of love at first sight again appears in Oliver's love for Aliena. In Lodge's *Rosalynde*, Aliena fell in love only after the hero's older brother had rescued her from a gang of thieves. Here we have what seems like an obligatory pairing; even Orlando asks wonderingly, "Is't possible?" However it is also a union with a number of precedents. Rosalind and Orlando also fell in love at first sight, and Phebe became similarly enchanted at her first encounter with Ganymede.

The comic confusion resulting from Rosalind's disguise reaches a climax in Scene II. Much of the humor in this scene lies in repetition. Each of the lovers reprises his or her declaration of love until finally Rosalind wearies of their "howling" and promises a solution to everyone's problems. She has enjoyed the opportunity to have a last bit of fun with her masculine identity, but now she knows that the masquerade must end the next day.

Note the contrast between "It was a Lover and his Lass" in Scene 3 and Amiens's songs in the second act. Here there are no allusions to winter and rough weather; it is a song of spring and young love, with subtle evocations of the theme of time. This song sets the tone for the wedding scene that follows; each lover will be paired with his lass in joyous finale.

Act V, Scene IV (pages 73–78)

New Characters:

Hymen: *the god of marriage*

Jaques de Boys: *second son of the late Sir Rowland de Boys; brother of Oliver and Orlando*

Summary

The next day, Duke Senior, Amiens, Jaques, Orlando, Oliver, and Aliena gather in the forest. Duke Senior asks Orlando whether he feels Ganymede can do all he has promised. Orlando replies that he has been wavering between belief and disbelief; he is afraid of being disappointed. Rosalind, still disguised as

Ganymede, enters with Silvius and Phebe and asks those who have assembled to have patience while she confirms that everyone has agreed to keep their promises. Duke Senior pledges his permission for Rosalind to marry Orlando if Rosalind appears. Orlando declares that he will marry Rosalind. Phebe says she will marry Ganymede if "he" is willing, but she promises if for any reason she decides not to marry Ganymede she will marry Silvius, who quickly agrees to marry Phebe if she will have him. Rosalind reaffirms her pledge to solve everyone's problems. After cautioning the lovers to "keep your word," she exits with Aliena. Duke Senior remarks that "I do remember in this shepherd boy/ Some lively touches of my daughter's favor." Orlando comments to the Duke that the first time he saw Ganymede he thought "he" was "a brother to your daughter." However he insists that Ganymede is "forest-born."

Touchstone and Audrey enter, and Jaques observes that there seems to be a flood in store, for couples are arriving two by two as they did when the Biblical Noah built his ark. Touchstone and Audrey, he remarks, seem "a pair of very strange beasts, which in all tongues are known as fools." Jaques tells Duke Senior that Touchstone has claimed to have been a courtier. Touchstone immediately retorts that if anyone doubts his word, they may put him to the test. At Jaques' prodding, he launches into witty discourses on the habits of courtiers, their quarrelsome natures, and the seven types of lies they practice. Duke Senior, pleased with Touchstone's wit, agrees with Jaques' observation that Touchstone is "a rare fellow."

Rosalind and Celia, now dressed in feminine attire, enter along with Hymen, the god of marriage. Soft music is heard, and Hymen asks Duke Senior to receive his daughter. Rosalind gives herself, in turn, to her father and to Orlando, and Phebe comments that "If sight and shape be true,/ Why then, my love adieu!" Hymen remarks that confusion has now been brought to an end, and that it is time to "make conclusion/ Of these most strange events." The four pairs of lovers join hands, and Hymen blesses their union. A joyous wedding song follows. Duke Senior welcomes Celia, and Phebe pledges herself to Silvius.

The wedding festivities are interrupted by the sudden

entrance of Jaques de Boys, the second son of the late Sir Rowland. He brings the news that Duke Frederick, having learned that every day "men of great worth" were fleeing into the forest of Arden, had raised an army and headed toward the forest with the intention of killing Duke Senior. When Duke Frederick arrived on the outskirts of the forest, however, he met an old religious hermit. After speaking with the hermit, Duke Frederick decided to abandon his deadly mission and forsake the world for a religious life. He also restored his dukedom to his banished brother.

Duke Senior is overjoyed at this news. He welcomes Jaques de Boys and remarks that he has brought additional happiness to his brothers' wedding. He pledges to restore to Oliver the lands Duke Frederick had confiscated, and he names Orlando as his heir. He also promises that the courtiers who have joined him in his exile will share in his good fortune when he returns to his dukedom. He calls for music and a wedding dance.

Only Jaques does not share in the festive spirit. He tells Duke Senior that he plans to join Duke Frederick in an austere religious life, remarking that "Out of these convertites/ There is much matter to be heard and learned." Jaques bestows his blessings upon Duke Senior, Orlando, Oliver, and Silvius, but he cautions Touchstone that his marriage to Audrey is likely to last only two months. He announces his intention to leave the wedding festivities, commenting, "I am for other than for dancing measures." Duke Senior pleads for Jaques to remain, but Jaques refuses, telling the Duke he will find a home in Duke Senior's abandoned cave. He exits, and Duke Senior gives the instruction for the couples to begin their joyous wedding dance.

Analysis

In spite of Orlando's skepticism at the beginning of the scene, everything is happily resolved. While waiting for Rosalind's inevitable entrance, this time in feminine clothes, we are treated to one last debate on the virtues of city life versus country life. Touchstone wittily describes the affectations one might encounter at court: flattery, craftiness, expensive clothing, quarreling. The quarrels he depicts are governed by set rules; the same holds true for the degrees of the lies told by courtiers.

Critics differ in their views of Touchstone in this scene. Some commentators feel that his vein is still satirical: he parodies the language of the affected courtier and burlesques a courtly due. Other critics are of the opinion that Touchstone's remarks are ironic, and that he is clearly "putting on airs." In Act I, Scene II, Rosalind called Touchstone "Nature's natural," but some observers feel that life in the forest has transformed this witty fool; he is no longer a critic of courtly manners, but rather their staunch defender. Either way, Touchstone's extended flights of rhetoric serve a practical dramatic purpose: they give Ganymede and Aliena time to change their costumes and emerge once again as Rosalind and Celia.

In classical mythology, Hymen was the god of marriage. The name of the god symbolizes the impending consummation of the marriages that will take place. Here, it is interesting to note that in ancient Greek dramas, plays were often resolved by what was known as a *deus ex machina*, literally, a "god from the machine." When mortals were unable to solve their problems, a god was lowered to the stage at a climactic moment to resolve the action—a convention Shakespeare would have been aware of. In this instance, however, the god does not solve the problems of the lovers but merely solemnizes their wedding festivities. Those onstage might well assume that Hymen represents the "magic" that Ganymede has promised; indeed, we are told that "Hymen from heaven" has brought Rosalind. But the audience (or the reader) is aware that it is Rosalind, rather than Hymen, who has brought an end to the "confusion."

With the entrance of Hymen, the play becomes a masque—a popular court entertainment in Shakespeare's time. Masques were usually characterized by music, dancing, and the appearance of supernatural or mythological personages. They featured far less plot than a play, and much of their impact was visual. Generally speaking, masques were allegorical in nature and took as their theme an idealized vision of the power of the reigning monarch and the ruler's divine right to govern. The masque of Hymen serves much the same function. Order has been restored to the proceedings; the chaos brought about when Duke Frederick usurped his brother's dukedom is resolved almost immediately after the wedding song.

In Jaques de Boys' tale of Duke Frederick's encounter with the "old religious man" we see the same type of miraculous conversion we had witnessed earlier in Oliver's transformation. If anything, Duke Frederick's sudden metamorphosis seems more implausible. Still, it is in keeping with the fairy tale nature of much of the play.

There are a number of ironies in the play's resolution. Note that Duke Senior, who has praised the pastoral life, plans a return to the court as soon as the opportunity presents itself. Yet Jaques, who has criticized life in the forest, chooses to remain.

At the end of the play, the caprices of fortune have been corrected; those of good nature have been rewarded, and those who were of evil nature have seen the error of their ways. All are not content, however. Jaques' decision to forego the wedding merrymaking and join Duke Frederick in a religious order lends a jarring note to the festivities, although it is one we might have expected from such a character. Yet his curiosity about Duke Frederick and his new way of life seems genuine, and it is easy to imagine that he well find satisfaction in his company. The ending of the play is by no means completely symmetrical, but the final scene concludes in a joyous spirit of communion and celebration.

Epilogue (page 79)

Summary

After the wedding dance, Rosalind steps forward and addresses the audience. She comments that a good play needs no epilogue, just as a good wine needs no bush—a reference to the ivy bush vintners in Shakespeare's time used on signs of their trade. Yet she argues that even good plays can be improved with the help of good epilogues. She apologizes for not being a good epilogue, and adds that she cannot slyly gain the audience's approval, for she is not dressed like a beggar; thus, it is improper to plead for an ovation. Instead, she will "conjure" the audience into applause. She addresses the women in the audience, telling them "for the love you bear to men, to like as much

of this play that please you." To the men she comments that she
hopes the play has pleased them as well. "If I were a woman," she
remarks, "I would kiss as many of you as had beards that pleased
me." She adds that she would like as many of the men "as have
good beards, or good faces, or sweet breaths" to applaud when
she curtsies and exits.

Analysis

In Shakespeare's time, of course, the role of Rosalind was
acted by a young man. Rosalind, in expressing the hope that the
audience has enjoyed the play, humorously acknowledges this
fact. Her reference to conjuring recalls her fanciful tale of being
trained by a sorcerer and the "magic" she promises and delivers
at the end of the play. Her comments are self-effacing, yet at the
same time they appeal to the audience's vanity. If all the women
in the audience who liked part of the play and all the men who
felt they had "good beards, or good faces, or sweet breaths,"
responded to her entreaties, she would have been greeted at her
exit by a hearty round of applause.

Study Questions

1. How old is William?

2. What does Touchstone threaten to do if William does not
   relinquish his claim to Audrey?

3. Who does Oliver fall in love with?

4. When does Oliver plan to be married?

5. When does Touchstone tell Audrey they will be married?

6. Who delivers the news of Duke Frederick's conversion?

7. Who was responsible for Duke Frederick's sudden change
   of heart?

8. Who does Duke Senior name as heir to his newly restored
   dukedom?

9. What reason does Jaques give for departing the wedding
   festivities?

10. Who speaks the epilogue of the play?

EPILOGUE

Answers

1.   William tells Touchstone he is twenty-five.

2.   Touchstone claims he will kill William "a hundred and fifty ways."

3.   Oliver falls in love with Celia in her Aliena disguise.

4.   Orlando tells Oliver that the wedding will take place the next day.

5.   Touchstone tells Audrey that they, too, will be married the next day.

6.   Jaques de Boys, the second son of the late Sir Rowland, delivers the news of Duke Frederick's miraculous conversion.

7.   Duke Frederick abandoned his plan to capture and kill his brother after meeting "an old religious man" on the outskirts of the forest.

8.   Duke Senior names Orlando as his heir.

9.   Jaques tells Duke Senior, "I am for other than for dancing measures."

10. Rosalind speaks the epilogue.

Suggested Essay Topics

1.   Compare and contrast the realistically drawn rural characters Corin, William, and Audrey to Silvius and Phebe, who are many ways the conventional "poetic shepherds" of pastoral romance.

2.   Explore the ways that Touchstone's behavior differs when he is in the company of "city" and "country" characters.

3.   Discuss the role of Jaques in the play and the reasons that may underlie his decision to remain in the forest.

4.   Explain the reasons why Duke Senior, after praising the pastoral life, might want to return to the court.

SECTION SEVEN

Bibliography

Barber, C. L. *Shakespeare's Festive Comedy*. Princeton: Princeton University Press, 1959.

Bloom, Harold, ed. *Major Literary Characters: Rosalind*. New York: Chelsea House, 1992.

Bloom, Harold, ed. *Modern Critical Interpretation: William Shakespeare's As You Like It*. New York: Chelsea House, 1988.

Campbell, Oscar James and Edward G. Quinn, eds. *The Reader's Encyclopedia of Shakespeare*. New York: Crowell, 1966.

Derrick, Patti S. "Rosalind and the Nineteenth-Century Woman: Four Stage Interpretations." *Theatre Survey* 26 (November 1985), 143–162.

French, Marilyn. *Shakespeare's Division of Experience*. New York: Summit Books, 1981.

Grebanier, Bernard. *Then Came Each Actor*. New York: David McKay, 1975.

Halio, Jay L. and Barbara C. Millard. *As You Like It: An Annotated Bibliography*, 1940–1980. New York: Garland, 1985.

Kott, Jan. *Shakespeare Our Contemporary*. Trans. Boleslaw Taborski. Rev. ed. Garden City, NY: Anchor Books, 1966.

McFarland, Thomas. *Shakespeare's Pastoral Comedy*. Chapel Hill: University of North Carolina Press, 1972.

Odell, G. C. D. *Shakespeare from Betterton to Irving*. 2 vols. New York: Scribner's, 1920.

Parrott, Thomas M. *Shakespearean Comedy*. New York: Russell & Russell, 1962.

Partridge, Eric. *Shakespeare's Bawdy*. Rev. ed. New York: Dutton, 1969.

Reynolds, Peter. *Penguin Critical Studies: As You Like It*. London: Penguin, 1988.

Shaw, John. "Fortune and Nature in 'As You Like It.'" *Shakespeare Quarterly* 6 (1955), 45–50.

Speaight, Robert. *Shakespeare On the Stage*. Boston: Little, Brown, 1973.

Ward, John Powell. *Twayne's New Critical Introductions to Shakespeare: As You Like It*. New York: Twayne, 1992.

Wilson, Edwin, ed. *Shaw on Shakespeare*. New York: Dutton, 1961.

Wilson, John Dover. *Shakespeare's Happy Comedies*. Evanston, Il: Northwestern University Press, 1962.